My Life in a Letter

One man's look at his memories.
Vol 1

SHABBAFRET

authorHOUSE'

AuthorHouse™ UK
1663 Liberty Drive
Bloomington, IN 47403 USA
www.authorhouse.co.uk
Phone: UK TFN: 0800 0148641 (Toll Free inside the UK)
*   UK Local: (02) 0369 56322 (+44 20 3695 6322 from outside the UK)*

Published by AuthorHouse 02/23/2024

ISBN: 979-8-8230-8343-0 (sc)
ISBN: 979-8-8230-8344-7 (e)

Library of Congress Control Number: 2023911936

Print information available on the last page.

Any people depicted in stock imagery provided by Getty Images are models,
and such images are being used for illustrative purposes only.
Certain stock imagery © Getty Images.

This book is printed on acid-free paper.

Contents

Chapter 1
First Memories

I was maybe six years old. The sun was shining; it was a Sunday afternoon. Dad and Mum had come back from the working men's club after a game of bingo. Dad was outside, asleep, sunbathing on a blanket from the lounge that we called the sicky blanket. Ironically, my dad was never sick even if he were, we would never know, old-fashioned in many ways that man. We didn't have quilts then on the beds; we had blankets so heavy that when you were under them, you couldn't breathe, let alone move around. Maybe that is why I don't toss and turn in bed now. There were so many of us that it seemed like there was always some noise, shouting, and arguments. I was the youngest of six (the spoiled one). I am not sure that is true; I am. I am more like the one who watched everyone else get a stern no and work out how to play the game, mostly with my mum, to get some of the things I wanted. Mum was so tired all the time, it was easy for me. I would pick my moments normally when we were alone, well when she, at last, had a moment when she wasn't doing the washing or picking up after "us lot", as she would often say or some other task to keep the house running as best she could, without much help from any of us kids mind, I would go up to her and make up some story about something I needed looking for some money mostly. She would say she couldn't. Then, I would say that she didn't care. Even Dad said he would if he could, but he said I had to ask you. My best line. Mum would get angry a lot of times. Not only was I asking her to give me some of the money she found hard to get from dad for her cigarettes, but because she was being disturbed in her alone time. I would go on and on, and often, she would give in just to shut me up whining and get back to her (me time). Then, sometimes, she would stay angry, and I knew I wouldn't get whatever I wanted at that time. That did not happen often, as I was getting better and better at it. Even though he tried not to show it, my dad had his favourites, mostly my eldest sister, Mary, the firstborn 12 years older than me (daddy's girl). Whenever we said anything remotely hurtful or spiteful about Dad, she would stick up for him to exhaustion, even if we were right. If only I could love someone as much, I thought Daddy's girl, Daddy's girl, I would call her that a lot. It would make her mad, and that's what I wanted. I was quick and thought she would never be able to catch me until one day, she did. I thought twice about calling her daddy's girl after that. Then there was Dawn, who was ten years old. older, now she loved everyone and everything. It seemed to me that she was quite easy to get on your side; this I found out quite quickly. I would fake being upset, and she would say some soothing words, and sometimes, before she left the house to get married, she would give me 10 pence to make me feel better. I was good at this. Her world was all about helping one another. That's what she thought, not in a practical way but in a comforting way. She wrote everything down in her diary, not a lot, just a few lines (she still does it now) every day from who knows when, maybe when at the point when starting to write (and is ancient now), but was good at drawing or was it painting, don't remember one time after school came in and proudly told everyone that her artwork had got an A STAR, (I never got one of these no surprise there) she got a well done from mum not a lot more from dad, a load of ribbing from Andrew, there was something of a shock for her from me, I wanted to know more, about was it in her form room, or was it hung in the hall for everyone to see Blah Blah, of course I didn't care it was just a way of setting her up for the next 10p I would get. I think she wrote a lot about it in her diary, maybe a dozen or so lines or even maybe a whole page; who knows, I never wanted to find it, although I did see it once, it was boring to me; then there was Joan she was nine years older than me, a complete opposite of Dawn. "Maybe the milkman's, we used to say." Then we would have to run. She would clout anyone (not Dad, obviously). But try getting Joan too and help with anything for anyone (good look with that), mum or anyone else. Joan was the nasty one who had my dad in her. We used to say the milkman must be her dad. but to call her that would wind her up. Family's Hey, we had to have fun wherever we could. A lot of the time, it was at another sibling's expense. Then Andrew, my only brother, is 7 yrs. older brothers can be close, that's what they say, especially if there were only two with (or if you like) against four girls in the same family, but we weren't close. I guess it may have been too big an age difference. He had his friends; they didn't want a little kid who was nearly half their age hanging around. My sister Julie was four years older than me. the closest in those early years, we spent time together, she was the closest to my age, I suppose, mostly we spent a lot of time in the house arguing, Mother Julie; I called her, and a lot of things besides, and yes to get her back up, anything for a reaction (that's one of my motto's). I was to find out many years later that she told me why there was such an age gap between me and her (it shocked me and had a massive effect on my sense of worth). She said mum got pregnant again only two years after she was born, but in mum's eyes, another child was just too much to bear. We were poor; Dad worked as much as he could and kept the finances in check; Mum worked too, but not in the early days. She had too much to do at home being "a housewife" (As they would call it then). Make the home a happy place for your husband to come home to; do not bombard him with questions as soon as he walks through the door, have his slippers ready and his dinner on the table, and make sure the children are quiet. these adverts on the TV said, thinking of those adverts now, makes me laugh out loud, the people they targeted had never seen our house at any time of the day, one-word MAYHAM. So, to find out as a teenager that there was a child between Julie and me and that my mum drank so much "on purpose" that she miscarried was a shock, to say the least, but worse is that she tried the same when she got pregnant with me, for some reason it didn't work. It's amazing to think that one moment could stop so much. My whole life would not have been here, and everyone I met, teachers' friends, the children I would have, even the people I bought a house from this book wouldn't have been here. Now, there's a black hole. If you think about that, it goes so very deep. What about the one that didn't make it? What would that child become, and how many lives would that child change? Mum and Dad would stop when they had a boy, but Julie came along. Someone said that Julie was a mistake before I discovered the whole story. Not sure where it came from. Someone must have said it (probably the ever-jovial Andrew). That upset her a lot, but what does that make me? Another mistake or something worse. They said Dad only had to put his trousers on the bed beside Mum, and she would get pregnant. That was about the time when Mum had so many problems; money was tight, very tight Mum smoked (too much and would pay for this later) and drank a little too at that time, but the Booze would raise its horrible, painful head later in her world, dad was always making her wait for a new supply of fags even though he smoked not as much as mum he gave up because of the cost rising, Never letting mum forget that every time he supplied her with a new packet. It was the way in our house. Dad earned money, the breadwinner, so it was his to spend as he saw fit and to be fair, that was mostly on the family's needs, although we always needed more. Mum used to go down to do the weekly shop and bring us all a Mars bar to share, and we all used to get excited about when she would come back and we could have a piece. Although it was the smallest piece in the world, it was so nice, and we all made it last as long as we could. Mary would oversee cutting it, so I never got an end piece, and neither did Andrew. However, there was always the "your bit is bigger than my bit argument. it had such thick chocolate and was much longer and wider than any Mars bar you can buy now. they started reducing it because Dad would say it's not as big as it was when he was a kid, not that he ever had one. We didn't know how lucky we were and didn't feel lucky looking at the tiny bit of Mars bar in my hand. There was no such thing as chocolate then as it was in the Dark Ages. Dad didn't mind this kind of joke sometimes, but you knew it if he didn't like you talking back to him. When I was a bit older, I remember going down to the co-op store every Friday with Mum to get the week's food; there weren't any supermarkets, just the local shop supermarkets. What were they? We had a meat counter in our local coop; what more would you need? though we didn't use it much, I Remember many a time going down to the butchers, a little shop in the Village, on a Sat morning to get the beef joint for Sunday dinner; one time Andrew came as we had to pay the tab they let us run up a few for a few meals worth of meat. Still, Dad always told Mum not to do it as he didn't like to owe anyone anything. Mum did this sometimes to keep the money he gave her that week for the meat to get more Fags. Every time we went, the butcher would ask if we wanted our bacon lean, as Dad used to have a couple of rashers for his Sunday breakfast. He didn't like the lean ones because they were more expensive, but he also liked the taste of the normal smoked ones. We weren't allowed any of that bacon. Good grief, no, we were lucky to get the rind of the bacon if there was any he didn't want, and Julie pretty much used to beg for it, that's if I was out of bed that early on a Sunday. The day the joker "Andrew" and I went down there, the butcher asked about the bacon. Lean? "He asked; Andrew duly replied, tilting to one side. "No thanks", he said. I think I laughed all the way home or for a good while. So, on a Friday, Dad gave Mum money that he thought she needed, but Mum was smart. She asked for a little more so she could sneak a couple of extra packets of cigarettes into the shopping basket. Dad knew, I think, but didn't say anything. If he asked for the receipt, Mum mostly forgot to ask for one; she used to tell him, but Dad never pushed her on it. She mostly kept the change in the money he gave her. Always giving him some back, well offering, he liked the thought of mum being economical with the money. yes, economical, alright, she always kept a bit back for, yep, more fags. Mum used to get us a small pack of sweets, Rolo's, or spangles.' oh, remember them? it was an ideal time to get a little bit extra. She used to give in to me, maybe to keep my mouth shut about her buying the fags. I got some sweets mainly, or a little pack of something that would last, like a pair of drops or cola cubes. Sometimes, I had to get a small chocolate bar like a "Fredo" and eat it before I got home because the other siblings were suspicious. However, it got a lot better when the country went green shield stamp crazy. You got them from everywhere: petrol stations, shops, even the butchers and the milkman (co-op milkman, of course). He gave us a few, I think, and the best thing was Mum could spend them in the co-op; I used to hide a few every week, and when I had a book full of the stuff I got from the co-op, she might not have got a receipt for Dad. Still, she never forgot her green shield stamps. Dad came to pick us up in his Morris Miner car every week. Even though it was only a ten-minute walk away, there were a lot of bags to feed the six little pigs in my family. I still remember the number plate NRD74; it must have taken 3 miles before the heater got warm when it was cold. Dad had green shield stamps in his car. I used to have a few of them when I could before he gave them to Mum. His work buddies sometimes gave him their stamps as thanks for taking them to cricket or picking them up for work when their cars were in the menders. It seemed Like he was always doing something for others, from building work to taking them here and there. But we had a new thing to do: stick the green shield stamps in the book. Mum got maybe two, sometimes three books from the weekly shop, and it was a way of getting something for nothing, it seemed; each one was worth £1, I think it was. If you think the whole shopping trip cost maybe £30, that was a lot. It used to take me quite a while to get a full book, but when I did, Paul, who would become my best mate, we could buy enough stuff to make us sick for a couple of days. The people in the co-op would not care too much. They knew; one time, however, one of the older shop workers, Margret, asked Mum how the party went. Mum asked what party and she told mum I had said we were having a party and that's why we bought so many sweets. I was quick with reasons or excuses. Mum scolded me about this. Outside, it was so hot waiting for Dad. I remember the frozen stuff was melting as Dad approached the bottom of the road in the old grey car. We had hot summers and cold, snowy winters in those early years. One year, I was still young, about 8. The snow was above the door, and when my sister opened it, a wall of snow stood. I was confused and a bit scared as Joan said we are snowed in now and will never get out. Then my brother Andrew went up to the snow, pushed through it, and fell into a heap with all the snow on top of him. It was not that compact. It was the fine drifting snow. It's amusing, though. He got up with snow all over his thick, wiry, curly hair (I didn't know it then), but I so wanted hair like that, and still do even now, with the snow in his hair and the snow around his face. Judy shouted, "Santa) Andrew was the joker of the pack, always trying to make people laugh; he did things like knock on the door, open it and shout to Mum that the invisible man was there to see her, then turn back to the door and said, Sorry, Mum cannot see you Today and shut the door, he was sometimes hilarious, But the summers were just as hot as the winters were cold. My dad loved the sun, so my memories of him lying on the blanket on the grass in the back garden are easy to remember and remembered with a smile one of these days, Julie. I was playing with a balloon with water tied up at the top and made a great swishing Sloshing sound, ready to pop if dropped or not caught. The Beatles were playing on the radio, and the twin-tub washing machine was on. There's a surprise; it seemed like it was always on. We were trying to be quiet but not managing it when running around, Mum shouting in an ordering kind of way, telling us to shut up shouting and to be careful not to disturb my dad on the blanket outside; normally, he had a few beers at the working men's club at dinnertime and would want a nap, Julie was Daring me to throw the balloon to her over dads sleeping body. I tossed the balloon up in the air, pretending to throw it, and the one time I did throw it, I didn't think she was ready. Splat, Julie dropped it, and it splashed onto my dad. We were horrified and scared, Trying not to laugh then remembering to run, yeah move, run away, running fast, away from him and his angry snarl, trouble was through the house wasn't very big and was only so far we could run this was the first time I had ever seen my dad angry towards me, he was furious it frightened me so much that even Today I can feel the unease of not knowing if we were going to get clouted. He had hands the size of shovels, so anything I would find out later was better than a slap with them. I had seen him throw stuff around the house when angry and kick stuff. It wasn't the clout we got, but with a grab of the arms and a shake, he shouted, "This was all the relaxing time I had." Then, calmly and a bit scarily, he said, "With all of you kids running around, I don't get a minute of peace." he sure made us know we had just ruined his time. He then stormed off to nap in bed upstairs, like most Sunday afternoons after his dinner. Strangely, people call the time they eat their main meal different things. Some say lunch is midday, and dinner is late afternoon. There's an early evening meal as well. Breakfast and Brunch, we just said dinner is whatever time we eat the main meal. Mum said we best watch out when Dad comes for his tea. Tea in our house was leftovers from dinner heated up (bubble and squeak), but mostly, it was just some tinned fruit. Dad had this with bread and butter, the freak. Anyway, we did keep out of his way. Well, we tried our best, but it was quite hard as it was a small three-bed house, with one small kitchen with a drying rack above the boiler that always had some clothes on it. In the lounge are two three-seater sofas and a chair for Dad. We had barely enough room for the coffee table. It got replaced by a tiny 4-seater table in the bay window. There was only enough room for two chairs when Mary left to get married; I remember a magazine rack at the side of the sofa that I always seemed to catch my ankle on. It was just full of junk magazines; they were as old as me, probably. I used to lie on the floor with my feet under the TV with a cushion under my head, although that stopped a few years after Mary left. She had a child, a boy called Joe; they all would come around on Sundays for a bingo game at the working men's club. Mary Joe and John, her husband, would always stop for dinner. (Dad was mostly OK with this as it was for his darling Mary. There was a joke about my mum's mushy peas and Yorkshire pudding. sometimes, Dad didn't like them joking about the food they hadn't paid for, but for the most part, it was OK. Dad didn't like John too much, but like most people, Dad would tolerate them. That Yorkshire pudding was yummy (I had it with jam on for a pudding), and that was a treat. I didn't like jam much as we had to have it on sandwiches sometimes when there was nothing else; my brother used to have tomato ketchup and vinegar on a slice of bread. Yuck, soggy, yuck. But I did like the jam still on the Yorkshire pudding. My favourite was Blackberry; I'm not much of a strawberry jam fan, but I want it now. After dinner, I started watching TV on one of the three channels we only had back then. Black Beauty was on. I think it was about a very clever horse and family, a doctor. We didn't even have channel four then, let alone channel five or the hundreds we have now. So, with my feet under the TV stand and my head on a pillow, I watched TV (my favourite way to watch well it was). Meanwhile, Joe came walking into the lounge carrying a thick wooden poker that Mum used in the twin tub washing machine to push the clothes down under the water; that was bigger and much heavier than a rolling pin. Just as black beauty was finishing, the pain from my face to my brain was so intense I think I passed out for a second or two. I woke up with all sorts of pain and Noise. Joe had only used the poker to hit my nose like he was smashing a fly. he was only about four, but he swung that very well. Everyone in the room laughed as a family seemed to do but soon stopped when they saw the state of my face. Never called an ambulance, though, for you had to lose a limb. And since we never had a phone in the house, if there was a problem, we had to go two doors down and use theirs. They were fine about it, even if sometimes it was late at night that one of us was in trouble and had to get in touch. we would ring that number, and they would come up and tell Mum or Dad what the problem was or even let us go into their house and take the call. different times, they were always quick to come up and tell us that there was a call; it was amazing how friendly people were. That must have been annoying after a while, and at all sorts of hours of the day and night, six kids trying not to get themselves into trouble but failing and hoping that dad would come and sort us out. It was a small village with approximately 2,500 people (thousands more now). They combined three areas (boroughs, if you will) to make one. all in line with a main road going from one end to the other through the middle of each part. It would increase a lot during my formative years. They started building new schools, three new housing Estates, and a bypass. The bypass, though, was on a floodplain; many times, when there was major rain, we got floods, and the water used to rise above the pavement and work its way up to our house normally would stop around the house from which we borrowed the phone. The next Village used to have a stream that turned into almost a river and always burst its banks over the road, causing all sorts of problems. It was fun most of the time when I walked to school. I went to a junior school that was about 800 yards away. Looking out of the upstairs window, you could see the bell on the main roof; we all had to line up when that sounded. Everyone who wanted to go to the toilet went, whilst the others had to wait in line. The boy's toilet didn't even have a roof; it was a door to two sit-down toilets and a wall with a trough for the fluids. we all tried to wee over the top of the I never managed that; the girls' toilets had four sit-down toilets, and there would always be girls waiting to go in. Sometimes, the snow would be ankle-deep if no one put salt down. It must have been cold to sit on those iron loo seats. Once, I fell over and got soaked on the way to school. I couldn't go back home as there wasn't anyone at home. Mum went after I left; she got a lift to work. So, there I was, soaked to the skin when we lined up with the rain going to start again. That wouldn't have made much difference; we still had to line up. The headmaster spotted that I was soaked and marched me into school to get some dry clothes from the lost property. I would get teased about the clothes, although dry, not very well fitted, the trousers were not long enough and very tight, the jumper was too big, felt like twice as big, and I looked like the arms were long. Baboon, they called me, the T-shirt had more holes in it than my shoes, after school when I got home I threw them on the fire and got told off by mum.

Chapter 2
Painful Memories

Not only did I have many painful days growing up, not just because the things I always wanted were always out of reach. And all the bullying Pain, real pain like the poker on my face, like going up the wooden hill (stairs) on my knees; yes, I know, but we didn't have much to do, so we had to occupy our minds with weird stuff. Well, some of us did! But again, pain someone had left a drawing pin spike up on the last but one stair from the top just on the part where the stairs turn. Two stairs go up to the left to the landing, where there is a square with three doors, one in front of Mum and Dad's room. No Entry. The other rooms swapped and changed personnel when another child left the nest. When we were all still at home, the door to my left on the landing was the biggest room but only big enough for one double and one single bed. So, the eldest Mary (dad's fav) had the single in the same room. Dawn, Joan, and Julie had to share the double, which was a double, not a king-size. Later, I learned that Julie used to keep getting kicked in the night as she slept well. tried to sleep, but she had to sleep between Dawn and Joan. And I'm assuming it wasn't Dawn, probably Joan, good old sisters. It wouldn't be much better for me if you turned right on the landing, with the door that never really shut because it never really fit in the door frame; this was the box room, and it was a box. I remember a steel frame bed, not quite a double bed size, that touched three walls and was off the floor but only just and if you got it wrong, it was high enough to take the skin off your shin. You could only open the door maybe halfway before it hit the bed. Andrew and I slept in this room. Trouble was for Andrew. I had icy feet and touched Andrew with them every night, sometimes on purpose. They were so cold it hurt, the best blankets and later quilts the girls had. We had the heavy-duty blankets; they made you feel like somebody had pinned you to the bed, which was very good for you. It can increase serotonin, a chemical that makes you feel happy and can help with poor sleepers. But not when your brother thinks he's playing in an FA Cup final, kicking the lower half of your body from one goal to the other. Happy times, not. So, near the top of the stairs, just before the last two steps went around the corner, there was the drawing pin with its shiny point of pain just waiting for the very young and soft flesh of my kneecap to kneel onto it. I screamed, but no one came running all normal in this madhouse; anyway, I was playing truant school, so no one was home. stood up and tried to put weight on my oh-so-stinging leg but couldn't. I had to hop and pick my leg up somehow without putting my other leg down in time, causing me to fall into the door in front of my mum and dad's room. Luckily, their door didn't have a perfect latch, so it opened as my face struck it, and I fell into a heap on the floor. I then looked at the pin with its shiny round head of pain looking back at me, and it said to my pain-ridden head, "You know you have got to pull me out; you cannot sit here. crying and waiting for mummy to come and make it better. So, I was in pain trying to pluck up from somewhere the courage to pull this thing out from just under my kneecap. I remember the pain of that splinter when I was trying to climb over the fence at the back of the garden to get my ball back. It would be a piece of cake. but try and tell my brain that every time I tried to grab hold of it, the horrible piece of wood moved a little and sent a shockwave of pain into my head. So, I had to hold onto this little round horror; if I kept letting go, it would never come out. There was nurse Julie. Yeah, I wouldn't give her the pleasure. I grabbed it in between my thumb and forefinger and held on as the pain shockwave went shooting to my head. pulled it stuck just for a milli second to give me that extra bolt of pain. This pain wasn't even worth calling pain. I'm unsure if it was even me hurting myself, but it felt like pain. But at least it was out of my knee. The spike of the pin was nowhere near the thickness of That splinter. It was the size and the thickness of my little finger. And I still have the scar Today. It went in just at the side of my bone under my knee, halfway down my leg. It's funny how you don't feel the pain at once. You know you have done something and can feel something wrong; with the pain starting to come, I looked down; wrong move. As soon as I did, the pain, oh my oh, the pain, it was like I had just had my leg chopped off. Half sticking out, looking like it was never going to be able to be pulled out, making me feel sick to look how far it went in, looking down the length disappearing into my leg, getting harder and harder to see the deeper it goes in. not really bleeding but hurting oh hurting so much. I walked well, didn't walk; it was. It is more like a hop, hop, hop, stager, hop, hop, stager. As I fell into the back door, whimpering and crying. Julie came in, trying to hold back the laughter and the potential enjoyment. She thought she was the family's nurse. She would not leave you alone if you got a big blackhead on your face, especially your nose; she had to squeeze that sucker. I did not want anyone to touch it, trying, hoping that if I left it, the thing would go away; I was so exhausted I collapsed on the sofa. I saw Julie coming over. I tried to get up and felt a sick pain, my body adjusting the temperature to help with any infection. Julie had other ideas. She forced me to sit still, saying she would sit on me if I moved. I wish I could just run away and hide, but all I could do was. lay on the couch with my leg throbbing she tried to pull it out with her fingers as soon as she touched it the pain doubled, I screamed at this point Andrew came in well to see what was going on then proceeded to hold me down, I was thrashing about big time hurting really hurting it now feels like someone is sawing my leg off with a blunt saw I was crying thought I was goanna pass out or even die from the pain very scared after several attempts and the pain getting worse with every try like the pin every grab of the splinter moved it felt like bending my bone grinding my bone, if that was possible and me screaming loud enough for the whole street to hear but they had all heard this family more than once, would they help maybe if the house was on fire they would, or maybe not, we were the family that didn't have anything, the parents in the street with families used to say if we haven't got it you don't need it to their own kids, boy we had nothing, No one would come running not just because of the screaming. My leg, the blood started to flow, and the two of them decided to speak out loud enough for me to hear that they would have to get the pliers from my dad's toolbox. I could feel another pang of sickness and pain; it was seemingly the same rhythm as my heart that I could feel pumping in my chest, and we needed something: an old towel to catch the blood. It was a lot more fun for them. Tim, our dog, came over to see what was happening, jumped onto the sofa, and sat on my legs as if to help Julie hold me down. He soon got off because I was kicking my legs like a wild stallion. He looked at me disgusted and returned to the corner near the fireplace. Nobody had lit the coal fire as it was hot outside; the hearth was nice and cool to lay on, so you would find him there on a sweltering hot day. He was not very well and wouldn't last much longer; he had a nasty rash on his back. It made him look horrible. His hair was falling out on his back, not shaved but so thin it looked so angry and sore; Andrew came back with the most sickening smile, waving the pliers around. Got them, he said in the most triumphant manner possible. I hate them; they love this, I braced, and before I knew it, they held my leg down and pulled the thing out of me. The pain went smashing through my leg, my stomach to my spine, my brain, and then back again, then relief, a deep breath but short-lived though as the blood flowed more than flowed, it was a lot. To make matters worse, Julie said there was some left inside. It would go mouldy and cause an infection, and my leg might drop off. I didn't hear that at first, but soon, I would worry about it for days and days, even asking Mum if it was true. After she told me more than a dozen times that it wasn't true, I started to believe her. On the stairs, I looked down at the pain from my knee from the pin and thought, I'm going to get a good bruise from that one. Any pain now is compared to when I lost the front wheel of my bike travelling down the road. all because I was showing off doing wheelies on my pedal bike. Lift the front wheel for as long as you can while riding. On one of the many occasions, I did this, my front wheel decided to come away from the bike. I wonder now if anyone had tampered with it, wouldn't be surprised, and go its way down the road. meanwhile, I was on one wheel, and the front of the bike was still in the air with the now vacant space where the wheel was just above the road. travelling fast, it seemed ages. I was getting tired and not able to hold the front wheel up. It came crashing down, and the forks that held the wheel in not very well hit the tarmac with some force; they were never the same again and would not be used much more after that or the bike. The metal forks hitting the floor started ringing into my ears when my left ear struck the ground. I was sliding and rolling down the road, realising that this was hurting and bleeding from the side of my face and my hands. It's funny how they always go down when you fall. And my knees took a lot of the impact but not as much as my shoulder. I couldn't make out that I was hurt as the other lads would surely take the mick. I was one of the ones they picked on anyway. The three brothers, Grim, my other mate, and I called them, were there, so as I was wiping the blood away and getting the grit out of the side of my face and shoulder, they took the mickey anyway. And I went home as gracefully as I could. A few days later, the bruise came out. I have never seen a bruise like it. it looked like somebody had painted my whole skin a wonderful purple, pink, black, and brown colour. Still, my six-pack was OK if it was there in the first place. There is lots of pain in different guises, from being kicked by Andrew and the bullying by the brothers Grim. Tim was going to the vet (the worst pain of them all).

Chapter 3
Bullying

The bullying never stopped until I left to go to Torquay when I was seventeen, still a teenager, a young 17 mind. Still, it seemed like heaven on earth for a while anyway. No one knew me when I had big ears, so they would not call me dumbo flapper or even dug less lug less. Even after an operation on them. but from an early age, I learned that if the bullying started, I would cry, and it stopped, well, most times anyway. makes me so mad to think that I never really stood up to all of them apart from one day I had just been kicked out of the house again for some reason or other. I saw one of them on his own, hardly ever on their own, so I put my head down and went to walk past. He started to call me names, came over and pushed me; I pushed him back and tried to punch him, caught him on his cheek. He went backwards, lost his balance, and sat on his arse. I was scared but happy and ran. He started to run after me, shouting he was going to get me. He soon stopped as he wasn't as good at running as me. When I was sure he wasn't around, I slowly walked to Paul's house. I met up with Paul most days. I told him he was my best mate, and he said I should have done it ages ago. I think he thought it was a full-on scrap, and when he went to school the next day, he found out it wasn't. He went to the same high school as them. I went to a newly built school to escape all the pushing and slaps I received when we all went to junior school. Our year got a choice to go to a new school in the village opening after the summer break. Or we go to the school in a village about 8 miles away and all must catch a bus. I knew what they were like when we went on trips and the teachers were there, so what would it be like when it was just us kids and the bus driver? So, I chose the new school as I knew the middle of the brothers my age would always go to that one as his older brother was already there. And they would all be together again the following year when the younger one attended that high school. But it didn't stop them from bullying me after school, but if I could avoid them, I did. I would not have to deal with them at school, so I spent half my life hiding in the shadows. but Paul went to that school with the brothers Grim. So, the day after, he asked the middle grim what happened, and he said, I ran away. He told Paul that no one would get away with saying that. We were going to have to fight at the park that night. If we didn't, they would be coming for me every day forever. Paul said I had no choice; if I didn't go, everyone would call me a chicken forever. He said just hit him like you did at the black pad. I said that the rest of them would be there. He said he would help if they stepped in. I knew he would not, but it was nice to hear. I had no choice; there were maybe a dozen kids there, as well as his brothers. Paul said to go up to him and punch him; even if you miss, at least you tried. They won't call you chicken, and yes, I did miss. I missed badly and nearly fell over. He hit me on the back of my head, and all I could do was cover my head after a few more hits with no reply. I was on the floor with a few kicks on my back and stomach from all three. I was making a crying sound, and they stopped. I got up, and he pushed and nearly pushed me over again. I can't fall over, I thought, as I would get kicked all over again; luckily, I didn't, and Paul walked away (I wanted to run, but Paul said no). I limped Away. Paul said that was shit, but at least you came. They may now leave you alone for a while, and they did, but not for long. Another guy went to the new school I got friendly with. The brothers grim knew him, and he went around with them sometimes, so I had seen him around when he told me they bullied him too. We hung out for a while. Paul came sometimes, but he was with a mate in another village that he hung around in the new school he went to and lived about 4 miles away. The guy had a brother who used to do banger racing (a load of old cars with scaffold poles in them in case they rolled,) and they did it often. Everything was taken out of the car, apart from the engine and driver's seat. They got battered, and after every qualifying round, if you weren't last, you had to somehow get it ready for the next round. By the time they got to the final race, there were more dents and pieces fallen off the car than was left on it, almost not recognisable, apart from the massive number on it and, of course, the name so that people could tell them apart, I went with him now and again then that stopped as the season stops Paul. I returned to how we were before this was always going to happen. Paul wasn't there when we met at the park once; I was waiting for Paul. I didn't do this often. The brothers grim could be around, and there they were. They forced me to play football. I had no choice, so I joined in. We were at the park playing football, and the tackles were flying in as always. One of the reasons I went in goal was that Paul was not there. Another of my mates got carried away with a tackle on the young brother grim. They made him pay in a not-so-nice way. They made him sit on the floor and jump over him, kicking him as they did. They turned to me and said it was my turn to do it to him; I said no. I got a couple of slaps and a kick in my shin. I hoped that hurt him as he grimaced. It hurt me it would be me next if I didn't. I looked at him, and he was crying, but he nodded, so I did, but I only just caught him and was made to do it again. I kicked him softly this time, but he made it look like I did it worse. They then let him go, and they went and took the ball; it didn't matter who it was. It was there now; we went to his house. He said it was not my fault, and they would have done it to me if I did not. It made me feel a little better, but not much. The number of times they just started on me and the number of times I made myself cry to get away without too much of a beating, like one time we were swinging over a small brook, with a piece of rope dangling and a stick tied to the bottom that you could jump up and sit on or hang onto it and lift your feet. That was fine, but you cannot keep your legs in the air for a while. Because they wouldn't let me get to either side, one on both sides pushing me back. One on the other, they made me drop into the water that was half water and half silt, that gooey muck that settled on the bottom of slow-moving water; it rose above my ankles over my shoes. They do these things just because they thought it was funny. I did not want to hang around with them and did not very often. Sometimes, we had no choice, and Paul kept us to ourselves. But on the odd occasion that they saw us, we had to. There were some payback times, though, once we were at the building site of the new housing estate. We used to jump off the first-floor scaffolding onto a pile of sand, but only after they made me do it first. to see if it was safe and if I hurt myself. This time, it was fine, but the younger one jumped a little too far and went over the top and right into some cat poo. He said if I laughed, I would eat it. I moved away and climbed back onto the scaffold. Then he went home. Another time, we were near the building site, but this time, we were messing about on a mud hill near a building site where they dug out the earth to build the new houses. It was about as high as a half-built house but as long as a football pitch in a curved shape, so if you had a bike, you could ride up one side and down the other. little dangerous as lots of bricks and holes, etc. I fell a couple of times, racing, as everyone did. But this one time, we went without our bikes. We set up on either side of the mound and started a game called crab apple bunging. That is what we called it. When you get a stick or, even better, a bendy twig with some whip, we would put one of the little apples on it and flick the stick, and the apple would fly a long way. The more whip of the stick, the further the apple would go. It was hard to aim. We did this up the park as there were loads of crab apples up there. It was an upgrade to snowball fights. There was not a lot of aiming, so it would be pure luck if it went anywhere near the target. But it would fly extremely fast past you sometimes. The trouble was there were only a few apples at the building site. We would round as many as possible into two piles, one at each end of the mound. However, there was no shortage of rocks and stones, so they started getting thrown. I hadn't started on them yet as I still had a few apples left; just then, an almighty scream of pain came from the other side of the mount. The oldest brother grim had blood coming down his face. It made me smile. I thought, I hope it hurts. Then, one of his brothers said somebody threw stones. Yeah, they were throwing them. I don't think Paul threw any, but you never know. They said that I did it. I showed them I still had apples left, but they were no good. I got the blame and had to run, so I picked up a dustbin lid, a metal one and ran; they started to throw stones at me; they hit the dustbin lid at the start, and two hit me on the back didn't hurt, but I felt it and got a bruise from one. The scary thing was the amount that hit the lid; it sounded so loud, and I nearly fell a few times but soon was out of range. I started laughing aloud pretty much all the way home. Paul, who was there, walked by my house soon after doing our sign to meet at the bottom of the road. I pretended not to see him. I saw him the next day, and he told me that the eldest brother was grim. He had his two front teeth broken and looked like a rabbit that had broken its teeth on something hard. I said a brick in the shape of a carrot. We laughed a lot at this. He never got them fixed, even now. I don't think he has a perfect arch in his two front teeth. He was weird-looking anyway. it just made him look weirder. So, we called him Bugs after that, not to his face, but it found its way to his ears. He chased us around the Village that day. We had a little hiding place we used to go to, not far from Paul's house. It was a little caravan near a load of apple trees we used to go scrumping (taking without asking). We thought they didn't know where it was. It was away from the road in an abandoned, overgrown land. The brothers grim were not the only person that bully you when people but soon after we had got there, he was outside banging on the door and windows and throwing things at the little two birth caravan that smelt like something had died but not gone to heaven, this caravan I think I had my first real feel of the opposite sex Paul was trying to go all the way with his really rather tall girl mine was her best mate, I got my hand inside her paints she wasn't ready to go this far and stopped kissing me well if you could call it kissing more like two fish that's too scared to touch lips more like two fish trying to eat each other so I was happy at how far I had got and went upstairs under her shirt there wasn't much up there and I think she was embarrassed because she grabbed my hand not before I felt the nipple go hard, I loved this it was the first time I had ever felt one so after a quick squeeze well more like a pinch I moved my hand, just then Paul was pushed off the seat well smelly cushion thing the tall girl shouted "NO I've told you before" and both stormed out. These girls had a name in the Village, that's all I will say they had less respect than we did, so the Monday when we went back to school it was all around the school she came out of the English lesson room at dinner time with a couple of her friends not with little miss very tall, I was walking by with my new friend one of her friend's said do you want to kiss her pushing her towards me, though because I have siblings I was a quick thinker I said why I would want to kiss her? Her friend said you didn't say that on Saturday in the caravan. I could see she was embarrassed. But I was in protection mode and said who will you believe? Someone like her or someone like me, we all know who she hangs around with. I walked away smiling but feeling a little sorry for her. She was a year younger than me, and I probably did nothing for her confidence. But after the fight in the park, pretty much everyone knew that I was a soft touch, an easy target, someone who wouldn't fight back, so I couldn't let the girls start winning. One early Sunday afternoon, I was walking with Paul the other way, and another lad, who was some cousin of the brothers, came towards us with his mate. As he walked by, I felt my face explode, blood streaming down my face. It was the only time I saw stars and thought I would black out. I heard Paul say something in my defence. He told Paul I would get a punch every time he saw me. The cut on my eyebrow would not stop bleeding, so as Mum and Dad were down the club, I went up to his house as everyone knew everyone, especially in the street of council houses that must have been 30 houses on my street a long road this with a slight uphill that seamed massive when we were small, with a big circle at the top (a ring we called it) like a mini roundabout without the small painted circle and had a pavement around both sides, I had been up to play at his house a few times.

His house was one at the ring set back and was one of the bigger ones, well longer anyway, five beds, I think, three doubles and two box rooms, but had a lot bigger garden. His mum liked me, and we always got on well. They were a big family of eight children, seven older than me, but the guy who hit me was a year or so younger. His mum was horrified and shouted for her husband to come, but he was in bed; that kind of thing happened often. Most men went to bed on a Sunday afternoon because of too much Booze. A couple of the older kids came in to see what the racket was all about. One of the girls said I'm going to kill him after she confirmed who it was, and she had just about finished patching me up when he came in. His mum went mad at him and smashed him around the face; he started to whale. He said it was an accident, don't lie, she said and hit him again, shouting at him that he was going to answer to Andy, the local policeman. This time, he would take him away. He was sobbing. Please, no; we were all a little bit scared of Andy as he was a no-nonsense copper and would not think twice about giving you a clip around the ear, let alone drag you back home if he caught you somewhere you shouldn't be like the building site. His mum said if you promise not to do this again and not to go anywhere near me. He went to his room, and I heard a load of shouting from upstairs somewhere. It must have been his older brother, as, like us, they would have had to share rooms; this was a blessing as he hardly ever spoke to me again after that. There were a few names and threats, but I always had the threat of Andy over him, so what a great idea it was to go to his house. Although I got a few slaps from his cousins, the brothers grim. I probably would have got them anyway. But he went to school with his cousins, which was perfect.

Chapter 4
School

There were few school memories as I did not enjoy it. I couldn't get engaged; they said I was too disruptive. They said no one realised, even me, that I was dyslexic. Now, there is a word to spell for someone who had problems with spelling and reading words; they never found out about this until the last year of school, as the country was learning about stuff like that. ADHD wasn't even a thing then, but I probably had that and other things as well. In my high school, the one that was only just built, the one I had chosen to go to, before the end of the last term, we could all go up to have a look so about 20 Eleven-year-olds went walking from main street to Station Road, it was only maybe ten minute's to walk but for an 11-year-old boy that wanted a wee so bad that I felt like my insides were going to burst. That journey seemed to take an hour. I thought about stopping behind a tree, but as I was not, shall we say, a well-behaved kid and had to be at the front with all the other disruptive, not trusted ones. the headmaster knew all about my family as all my siblings went there and got into trouble (all but Dawn), for something or other. Still, it was easy to get into trouble as the headmaster was a tyrant and got a thrill out of making kids feel stupid. For example, when one of my classmates did not know the answer to a question, he had told us about an hour ago. And the poor kid, because he was not listening, was made to stand in the corner facing the wall with a baby's rattle and a baby's dummy. He then had to turn around to us all and suck the dummy and shake the rattle for at least five minutes; we all laughed. Mostly, that was what the headmaster wanted. But pretty much everyone knew how that kid felt, so I would never leave the line and have a pee. God knows what he would do, probably tie me to the tree or something, so by the time I got to the new school, and he was talking about us being the first children ever to set foot into this place, funny I thought I had been here loads while they were building it, to see if there was anything I could have well borrow, as I told Andy once, I knew that the toilets were just down the hall opposite where we came in, so I positioned myself at the back of the group knowing I could easily slip away and pop into the toilets. What I didn't know, though, was that these toilets were the staff toilets, and my new headmaster, I soon found out, was in a stall straight in front of the second door into the actual toilet with the toilet door open; why would you even do that? I can never get that image out of my head. He was getting off the bowl to stand up as I burst into the toilet, almost wetting myself. I saw everything: the meat and two veg; all I will say is that man is very hairy. but my gaze was soon broken by his shouting. "BOY, GET OUT OF HERE GET TO MY OFFICE NOW!!" It made me forget I wanted to wee; thank God I could have lost my bladder crying with sheer panic. I ran out of the toilet and tried to rejoin the group, but it was no good; the shouting alerted everyone outside, apparently waiting for our new principal to give us the royal tour. He came out with a look on his face of absolute disdain. Oh great, we have another principal who doesn't like kids. My old headmaster grabbed me and, like a prisoner of war, handed me over to the new man in charge. It must be an unwritten code, I guess. He, in turn, grabbed my arm, another bruise to add to all the other ones, and dragged me away from the group to his office, where there was a smell of leather and pine newness; before I could even get that thought through my brain, he shook me and shouted again. "YOU, BOY, HAVE A LOT TO LEARN AND GOING WHERE YOU ARE NOT TO IS ONE. I WILL BE WATCHING YOU, BOY. YOU WILL BE IN MY FORM, SO I WILL BE ABLE TO WATCH YOU AND SEE YOU EVERY MORNING, SO THINK ABOUT IT THROUGH THE SUMMER; I WILL BE WAITING FOR YOU TO START NEXT YEAR. BE WARNED, IT'S NOT GOING TO BE A PICNIC, NOT FOR YOU ANYWAY!! Now, as calm as he was, I was not sure if this scared me anymore; he said now go and join the group; we are late at starting the tour; I don't like to be late. I have more than this one to do Today. I went back out and joined the group. and grabbed again. That will be another bruise, and I was frog-marched all through the tour, being pushed and pulled in and out of every room. Loving life, not! But I got the title of being the first kid to get told off at the new school even before it was fully open. I was so scared almost all summer when I thought about starting the new school. Mum had found me some of the uniform well colour schemes from jumble sales. They were black trousers and a blue or yellow top, so the trousers were fine, but the yellow top she got was horrible, but it was all I had. I covered it up with the strange blue colour jumper I got. The following year, we got given some clothes, probably out of lost property. The first day came. Mum was excited and took the day off work; it was an open day for all the parents to come and see the school. Then they left, and we went to class. In my first encounter with my nemeses, he shouted out everyone's name; one after the other, my name came out, and with a small voice, I said here. Speak up, boy he said. That shirt? Is that yellow? I said I thought so, then went on to the next name; I felt smug and got away with that. I thought when he finished calling all the names on his sheet. He looked at me; I gulped, repeated my name, and told me to stand; another feeling of sickness came into my throat. I didn't think I could hold onto it. He started saying if you came on the tour in this boys' group, you would know the story, but if not, I will tell you. It nearly made me cry, but I was determined not to cry in this new school, which was challenging. He went on. This boy went into places he shouldn't and saw things no one should see; laughter rang out. He said, if I find any of you going into the staff toilets, staff room, or other staff-only places, you will be in more trouble than you can imagine. Now sit down. again, you made me late by staring at me. It was a great start, but it got easier. I was good at getting people on my side, but he was never on my side. He left me alone after a while; for the most part, I kept my head down when he was around, and I was allowed to move class in the second year, thank goodness. The second year, I had a new best mate only at school, though as his parents were Mormons or someone said Jehovah's Witnesses, and he wasn't allowed out after school, well, not often. Sometimes, I would play in his garden, and he was allowed to play in ours. There were a few too many people in our gardens most of the time. We sometimes went to the park or just walked around the Village. It was always just after school for an hour, sometimes two, but I had to walk him home so his mum knew he was with me. I remember him eating bread, not butter, every chance he could. He said that it was what made him big and strong. I probably eat more bread now because of that. Paul wasn't out yet from school as he had to change and have his tea before coming out. he mostly had to be in by the time Paul was ready. The family didn't stay in the Village much longer after that and moved out in the middle of the third year; he never kept in touch, though; he was a bigger lad than me, much stronger and never took any messing from anyone, even the brothers grim. He would go up to them and punch them if they said anything. Even if they were all together, they sometimes tried to fight him, but he grabbed one of them and punched him, and they all soon backed off. I loved this, although he only had to do it a couple of times when pushed, and they would push him; he didn't care if there were one or three of them; he said he had to deal with people like that all his life. At the new school, the girls could not care less about us, and the tough guys were too busy fighting themselves to be bothered with us; fine by me. We had fun, though. The run-in with the headmaster wasn't the worst part of my high school life. There were a lot, but two others that were quite bad. One time, I wanted some docs, Doctor Martin boots. "Everyone had some." There was a lad in school who had some for sale, and I said I wanted them; he said it would cost me £8 bargain they were £20; they weren't brand new, far from it, but good enough, and I wanted them so bad, it was taking weeks to get the money together begging my sister borrowing the odd 50p giving him everything I had it wasn't that much, a couple of weeks went by he said things like he was going to sell them to someone else, I had to think fast we were in woodwork class. I never got to do much apart from a sleeping rabbit carved out of a block of wood because we had to pay for the wood if we wanted to take them home. I never did, but the rabbit did find its way home. Mum and Dad saw this carpentry marvel and said, "Flatly good, yes, perfect. In this one woodwork class, we all saw the glass jar where the teacher used to put the money the kids had paid to take their stuff home for some reason, probably so he could get more stock without going into the school budget. But we both saw the fiver the next day; he said if I get him the fiver, I could have the docs, so I would plan how to get the jar the next few days. I would watch him when he went on lunch, where he went and how long for, and if I took the lot jar and all, maybe I could leave the jar empty and take all the money, even the coins, or the fiver. There were a lot of coins in there, ten or more pounds worth. Anyway, one break time, I saw him put the jar in a cupboard and go off for dinner. I had half an hour I saw him going towards the staff room as he mostly did, apart from if he had to get his lunch from his car. Today, though, he went to the staff room, so in the cupboard, I went. The plan was to take it into the woodwork room with all the saws; this door was open, too. I looked at the jar and thought hard about taking the lot. Still, I had already told myself in the plan that I couldn't hide the jar. If I took the coins out, they would jingle in my pocket, so after what seemed like an age, I opened the jar, just took the fiver, and put it in my sock. I saw this on TV: that guy got away with it after being searched by the law. I also planned this. It was also in my planning. I quickly put the lid back on and put the jar back. I saw a girl walk past; she did not see me in the cupboard, but I thought she did anyway. It's too late now. I am on my way to get myself some. Doc Martine's, I still had to wait over the weekend as he didn't have them that day. But he wanted the money. I didn't want to give it to him, but he said he wouldn't bring the boots if I didn't give him the money first. That Monday was probably the only time I got to school early to meet him off his bus as he came from a different village. I would have walked to his house over the weekend, but I did not know where he lived. I knew the street, I think, but hey, I could wait, well, only just. He got off the bus, and I said, "Have you got them?" He gave them to me wrapped in newspaper. I tore this off. As I was doing this, the woodwork teacher got out of his car and looked at us. Oops, I thought and turned away to go inside, clutching my boots and smiling. to myself, I had Them. Come on, me, way to go, me. It didn't last that long, though, as in assembly that morning, the headmaster told the school that someone had stolen money out of the jar and they were going to call the police. I'm sure they were both looking at me. They all seemed to be looking at me, but then I noticed the girl who saw me near the cupboard. I looked away as I looked at her. Oh no, I thought she was going to tell them. What was I going to do now? I could only go home, hide the boots, and hope the cops didn't come around. I returned to school in time for the afternoon as we had woodwork, and I thought I had to go as they would know if I didn't. The teacher didn't seem bothered about the fiver, and I thought I had gotten away with it. I had to stay behind after the lesson was over; oh shit, I thought. The teacher was nice, saying we all want things in this life, but you must work for them and cannot take shortcuts to get what you want. It will always end in you failing; there is no easy way, just hard work, he said; the best part was that he would not call the police not until this time next week; he would leave an empty jar in the cupboard and if the five pounds appeared nothing else would happen. I had a chance to keep the boots. I need money. I need money. It seemed like everyone was talking about money, how much this cost, how much it was to go somewhere. I was worried and desperate; I had only got £1.90, which was all I had in the world. That wasn't mine. From when I didn't pay for some extra meet mum wanted me to get from the butcher. I told him to put it on the bill; she would never remember. I thought I had to have it; the family would probably ask for it back, especially Dad. He never forgot anything about money, but I had to have this and more. I was nowhere near the £5. It was Sunday night. I had no choice; I had to tell Mum. I said these shoes were on sale for the school charity and were only £5. I have £1:50, and she said there was no way I had £3:50 and that I would have to want them; how did you get the £1.50? Wait, I don't want to know she sighed. I went into the get what you want from mum mode, saying stuff like It's for charity. It's for little kids that have got even less than we have. That was a good one, and I threw it in for good measure. I won't ask for anything again, OK, she said a little too loud (probably knowing I wouldn't stop). When do you want the money, she said, sounding forlorn. I said tomorrow, or they will be gone. She said she saw and would talk in the morning. The next day she asked Dad for some money for fags he moaned like hell. He gave her the same old, going to be the death of you and the family. We won't eat if you keep spending all the money, but most of the time, he gave her a fiver and went into the toilet with his paper, like every morning. She turned to me after everyone else had gone to school and Dad had gone to work, said give me your £1:50 and take this, but do not ask for anything else this year. I entered school, and registration was about to start, so I knew the cupboard should be unguarded. It was. I put the fiver in the open jar; at least none of the kids would know I had taken it, but they all whispered it anyway, so I went to my class and got told off for being late, which is normal. That afternoon in the woodwork, the teacher said in my ear well done. It wasn't easy, but I hope I learned a lesson. I did for a while, but that sort of trouble. Seamed to follow me. The whispers got louder now everyone in the school knew, so I became a little bit mouthy and tried to be the joker; it was a clever way of getting through the rest of school. In the third year, I pushed a little hard, and the poor French teacher got me messing about big time. I liked French for a while but, as usual, got bored, so once, the teacher said we were having a bingo game. We should all put five numbers in a square in our books, and she would call out the numbers in French, and the one who won would get a MARS BAR. I had to win, so I came up with the idea that the whole class put the same five numbers down, and we should all get a Mars bar each. A couple of the girls were not keen, but some other boys made them by taking their pens and writing the five numbers in their books. Just in time, the French teacher came back with her Mars bar. The 12 or so kids all played bingo, and it was going so well, the teacher thought, until the number 21, Van urn. I think that's how you spell/say it. but when it came out, the whole class erupted, shouting different words for them winning bingo: here, house, me, I won, I said, oh miss, we all must have a Mars bar now; her face dropped, and she ran out of the classroom crying, most of us started laughing. Then, guess who had seen her in the hall crying? Yep, the principal. He came barging in. WHO DID THIS? WHO IS TO BLAME? Some turned to me, and one girl pointed. I pleaded it was only a joke. I got another bruise from the arm grab, marched again up to his office, and got the riot act read to me again. and made to sweep and clean the gym changing rooms. Sweaty smells were everywhere, and underwear hid in the strangest places. Who would leave their underwear? I tried to stay out of trouble at school anyway. I was off school for a while, so that was easy. I always had problems at school. I had problems with my ears sticking out and was always getting called names dumbo, big ears, and radar etc., I was always trying to hide them, but my hair was straight as a board and very thin. I wished I had hair like Andrew. Mum heard the chants, some even being called by my siblings. the doctor said they could do something about them and pin them back. OK, I was fine with it, but Mum told me that her operation for the same thing didn't work, and they popped back out again. Oh yeah, thanks, that helps, Mum. My operation was when they pinned my ears back to my head. It wasn't quite as straightforward as everyone had said. The Dr never told me the whole truth; they cut a circle in the back of my ear, bent the Cartlidge, and then had to stitch them back together and had me in a bandage for six weeks with a little bit of hair poking out of the top. During the time of the bandage from hell, I put a knitting needle through one of my ears. It hurt a lot, but the itching was driving me crazy. I pushed the knitting needle under the bandage and tried to itch my ear with it but only succeeded in putting it through my ear. When the bandage came off, my hair was like an afro, but it looked like I had just had an electric shock without the curls. Initially, I didn't mind much as I could scratch my ears and head and have a few more school days. The day I went back to school, some people commented. Not many; most couldn't care less. After a week or so, we had a science lesson, and the teacher was another one who did not like people messing about its dangers; he would say I was one to watch. This day, as we were waiting for him to unlock the science lab, he came prancing in like the cat that had got the cream, came by us in what can only be described as a salmon suit with bits of fluff on it. So, me being me, I could not keep my big mouth shut. I said in a very posh voice. "OH, MIND THE OLD SUIT OLD BEAN WHAT WHAT?" Suffice it to say he didn't like this, dragged me up to the front with one of my ears, and tried to pick me up with both ears. I was thrashing about, screaming, crying, panicking, and kicking so hard he let go. I kicked him and ran home, scared to death. My ears had come open and had a massive hole in the back. They hurt like hell, by the way. I wouldn't go to school after that; I didn't want to. I was afraid that something was going to happen to my ears. Mum kept saying they were fine, but I needed more than just Mum saying that, not only because Andrew and Julie told me my big ears would return when I woke up one morning. I would have holes as big as eggs on the back of them, and I would bleed to death. Mum and I went to the doctor to try to stop me worrying. The doctor said I had bruising but nothing to worry about and gave me some of that powder you mixed with water that seemed to get for every ailment. After a week or two, Mum dragged me up to the school and had it out with the principal; I was never prouder of Mum than that day. She told the principal in no uncertain terms that I would not be doing science again with that teacher. If he came near me or the other teachers touched my ears, she went straight to the school board and the police sighting assault. Well, this must have shocked him as about three weeks later, there was a new science teacher, and our classroom was now two; they asked if I would return to science with this new teacher. Mum said I should, so I did. I liked science. It was one of my favourite things with a little danger, like when he made a flower go brittle by putting it into something so cold it froze. I wanted to put loads of things in, like one of the girl's long hair, but I wasn't allowed. I'm not sure how long the other teacher was there for after that as I left high school that year and went to another school where the brothers grim never went so happy days.

Chapter 5
Bunking Off School

Not going to school, more and more things happen not to everybody, but they did to me. One day, I was watching a math program as there wasn't much to choose from. I didn't mind it, to be fair. It was a kind of science math. I was getting hungry; there was not a lot of choice. I would say in the fridge, but we didn't have one; we had a pantry, a cold storeroom with an outside wall, no heating, and stone shelves to put the stuff on. It had a curtain, a yellowish orange thing with no pattern, some old cloth from somewhere, a jumble sale. I suppose mum loved going to them. It's where we got most of our stuff from. The pantry worked not because it was cold enough but because its stuff was not there long enough to go off. Sometimes, though, the bread did start to grow Mold around the crust. We had to cut it out and still eat it, or we did not have bread. Same with the cheese, but Dad had that mostly, so it would never make the Iron Man fall ill; anyway, it's paracetamol, they now say, so he was so full of that the Germs never had a chance. Mary never takes the top slice even if it is her bread and it is fresh; I remember one year at Christmas, it's time. I moved the cloth door out of the way and reached around to get some bread. To my horror, a goose was hanging by a hook with a massive hole in its neck with a bowl catching any blood that dripped from the horrible-looking thing. It had most of its feathers still on, but the smell of blood was horrendous; when it was time to cook it, Dad had a go at plucking this huge bird but didn't do an excellent job. Mum had to take over, or it would never be ready for Christmas, she said; all I could hear for the next few hours was a sound like a snapping, ripping, crunching noise. But on this day, I made toast on the gas cooker grill. It was ancient and had an eye-level grill. The clicker that lit the gas never worked on the grill, so you had to turn it on one of the lower gas rings that did work with the clicker, then get a bit of the newspaper, roll it up and light that with that burning very fast you turned the grill on the gas pouring out then if the newspaper fire stick hadn't gone out you can light the grill. Still, the whoosh would send sparks of the paper all over the place, including towards your face. If the gas lighting didn't remove your eyebrows, the paper burns made up for it. So, I lit the grill and found two slightly mouldy slices of bread. If they had bits of mould on the crust, we always just cut off the crust and eat the rest of the bread as normal. Still, if the mould had spread onto the actual slice, we would think twice, but believe me, when you're hungry enough, even that won't stop you. This bread wasn't too bad. I put them under the grill and went back to the TV. I got so hooked on trying to solve this sum that I forgot about the toast until I smelt it burning, I thought in a mild panic now. Between the lounge and the kitchen were two glass doors that couldn't see through them as the pattern made it almost impossible. One was always open, and as one of the sofas backed up to it, I got up and raced toward the kitchen and, for some reason, known only to the stupidest people in the world. I jumped up when I reached the glass doors; maybe I meant to jump forward, not up. Still, I stupidly jumped up. The rest of my body moved forward as my forehead hit the top of the door frame. My legs flew out and upwards in front of me. My feet hit the ceiling, and I landed with a thump. I winded myself so bad and almost was knocked out seeing stars, as they say, and winded I could see smoke starting to come out of the grill after rolling around on the floor, somehow trying to get my breath back and ignoring the pain on my forehead and in my back, I got up onto my knees by the time I got to turn off the grill there was smoke billowing out of the grill I have had burnt toast before so I knew that I couldn't waste it and scrape the burnt off with a knife if it was too bad it used to break into pieces but still got some butter on them and ate them. These, on the other hand, were cremated; no amount of butter could save these rounds of burnt offerings. The smell lingered and lingered even though I opened all the doors; the front door and the back and windows front and back door kept slamming shut, which annoyed me, so I put a plant out from the toilet windowsill. It was called a Christmas cactus, or so one of my siblings said; it should flower every Christmas, and every Christmas, I was somewhat disappointed not to see it doing its job. the wind was too strong and blew that sucker over, creating a royal mess of bits of the plant. They were everywhere, the parts of the plant itself that looked like someone had stuck two oval green shapes together end to end in the soil; oh, it did take me a while to clear that mess up, with my dizziness starting to bruise head and back, I had to sit down a few times felt sick and almost was. Still, I had to clean it up before the rest came home. Do you think the plant rolling around the kitchen is why it never flowered? It could have been, I guess, Opps. Things like this happened when I was off school. Sometimes, my best mate would play truant too, not any of the brothers grim, the one mate that did not hurt me with names or physically and was more like a real friend, Paul. We stayed together for years and years. Even girlfriends did not have much chance to come between us for long. The walking kids, as we called ourselves, started to become inseparable. We walked everywhere. Swimming was 8 miles away, the nearest pool. The brothers grim came sometimes and tried to drown me by pushing me underwater. I got good at swimming and could go quickly over a short distance. So, when we played tig, I was quite safe. Well, in the water, anyway. because they would dunk me under if they did catch me. The walk back was always worse; someone would find something to tease me about, like You have had your weekly wash now, or My ears looked even bigger with my wet hair; I used to drop back. They had to get home for their tea before six. I didn't get any. If I did, it wouldn't be much. They stopped coming after a few weeks; It was much better. Sometimes, we had enough money to buy some things from the shop. Mostly, we brought a pack of biscuits called TUC biscuits. I did enjoy those days. Soon, it would stop, though, as a school would start again, and the summer holidays would be over. Mum used to call me to get me out of bed and come down before she went to work to make sure I got up and was getting ready for school. I was the last to leave the house and first to come back, so after she went, I went back to bed most days. It got so bad that the attendance officer used to come around quite often. I always hid. It was deviously scary; I wasn't the only one that played truant school. Julie also didn't like school; her so-called best mate was bullying her. Well, only mate, she used to be a real Bitch to Julie as she used to turn all the people Julie got friendly with against her and made her cry. like the brothers grim did to me. So, it's no surprise that she stayed out of school. We stayed off school for about three weeks solid, and one day, when Julie was mowing the lawn, the attendance officer came around. I didn't see her as I was in my bedroom, but it overlooked the garden, and I heard her say in a very mean and stern voice, if you are well enough to mow the lawn, you are well enough to come to school. So come on, young lady, get your things. You're coming with me. "PISS OFF," Julie said, running into the house and locking the door. If only she were that brave against her mate. Still, fear of one thing made you stronger towards another, especially if the other was going to hurt you, But I know how this feels and why we never do. Anything about the real things that cause us pain. Being scared is only in your mind, or is it a stronger self-preservation? There were some injuries at school with me and my I can do this way attitude. One time, the class was doing the high jump, and instead of doing it properly, I did it my way. I would run, stop, and jump up over the bar backwards. The teacher said it was in the rules as it was called the Fosbury flop. I got carried away, and yes, I hurt myself; the bar was a triangle shape. I know how stupid it was that I was getting the bar put higher and higher, clearing each height. Then I knocked the bar off, and it landed on the crash mat with my back heading for the bar; the momentum made me slide across the top of the triangle-shaped bar, and the crash mat helped to hold the bar in place as it ripped my back to shreds That did hurt. Still, I could not show it in front of the class, so by the time I went home, my shirt stuck to me with my blood; when I removed my shirt, it opened a lot of the cuts again. I once was running down to the field one dinner break, and there used to be steps of about five, so easy to jump; I used to do this a lot, one time. However, I tripped as I jumped and fell into a heap, my bag's contents everywhere, and pain in my knee, hand, and elbow ringing in my head. I looked up. Three girls were looking and sniggering. I picked up my things, put them in the bag, and walked around the corner, showing no sign that I was hurt, but then collapsed in a heap, rubbing all the pain like that was going to make it go away. It wasn't the worst, though. In PE, one time, we had the trampette out. It is a small trampoline that you could put at an angle, jump onto, and do star jumps or Tiss overs, as we call them. There were somersaults glorified forward rolls. Still in the air, the trick was to tuck your head in quickly and use the momentum to get you through the roll. It looked great when you did it correctly. I was particularly good at these exceptionally good. I had no fear, just plain stupidity. Yep, that is me, stupid to a fault when I could do something I thought I was ace; I love the attention. good attention, not the bad stuff I normally get. The teacher used to tell me to show the class how to do it right, so I did as I was so good at it. The trouble is I had tucked my head in far too early and smacked the back of my head on the high part of the trampette. I was knocked out for a short while and had to go to the sick room; they called my dad. It was only about midday, and Dad was not too pleased to have to leave work, which was his life, everyone knew. He came, and the head teacher told him I must go to the hospital, so begrudgingly, he took me to the hospital, moaning all the way. The doctor finally came and looked at me. I did not have a scan on my head, just this doctor with his hands all over my head, pressing down on the injured bit. He then told my dad to give him some painkillers and stop him from sleeping, and if he was sick, ring us. Dad shouted at him, "We have been here for over seven hours, and that is all you will say. If he were going to sleep, it would have been while he was waiting for you clowns; with that, he grabbed my arm, and we left.

Chapter 6
Accident

Paul and I would walk anywhere to parties and gatherings, thinking they were available girls. There maybe were, but never for us. nope, never for us. We were too immature to look at, let alone the way we acted, all very childish; we would not have any chat to talk to the girls. I was never confident enough to start the conversations. I was always getting my confidence knocked by all the name-calling because of my ears. I was skinny and not very tall, so I just looked weak that was also somewhat of a target for name-calling, as were my second-hand clothes; with the bullying, I didn't want to say boo to a goose, let alone try and talk to girls I could not stand the thought of rejection. We used to walk everywhere. We used to sometimes walk to Paul's school 8 miles is a lot. It usually took about an hour for him to go to registration to sign in to try and fool the school that he was there all day. Still, he would come out while I waited, and we would walk home again, normally going into mine or hanging around anything but going to school. It worked for a while, but the attendance officer got smart and, after a few months, would find Paul sneaking out. And take him back to school, so I must walk home alone. This one time, he never came out; I waited well over an hour because sometimes he had to go to his first lesson, which was about an hour long, then would meet me at the park near the school when he never came. I went home. I was thumbing a lift down the main road; it was safe then, and people would generally stop. It was normal to stop for people, even kids. Paul and I would say a gorgeous sex-mad woman would stop one day and make us have sex with her; sadly, that never happened; all sorts of people used thumb lifts. There were no problems, and people used to stop quite often, never a woman driver on their own, although we fantasised that they would. A red car stopped about thirty yards in front of me. As I walked up to the car, there was an almighty screech of brakes, the most sickening noise of metal hitting metal, and more tires stretching. I turned around, and a lorry hit a car. It was hard to tell with all the twisted metal wrapped around a tree on the other side of the road and the crushed side where the lorry had smashed into it. The front of the lorry had Jac knifed, that's what they called it. I froze. It was heading straight for me, and the red car just before me moved forward. I ran so fast that I almost passed the car. we stopped. I looked back. A car was in the hedge on the other side of the road. It didn't look like a car anymore. The car should have been white. But it was now more like a dirty grey colour. With the side smashed in, I could see the other side wrapped around the tree. and what looked like an arm or a leg hanging out with blood on the twisted metal. By this time, the lorry was in the ditch alongside the path on our side of the road with its trailer at a right angle across the road. The cars travelling behind the car and the lorry had stopped, and people were getting out to help. I remember seeing a dog jump out of the cab with the lorry driver. The car driver who had stopped to give me a lift said do you want a lift or what? There are enough people to help them, and they Will not need us. So, I got in, and he dropped me off at the lights on the main road at the top of the village. It would normally take me 20 minutes to walk this, as I have done many times. Every time a large vehicle bigger than a van came by me, I jumped in the hedge or got as far away from the road as I could; by the time I got onto my street, I was crying and shaking; it must have been shocking I guess I went into my house. I was sick. I don't remember if it was a lot, but there were carrots. Amazing, I didn't eat carrots. Later, Paul came around and walked by, and I called him in as the coast was clear, and no one was home. He had gotten out of school at dinner time and come home. And I told him all about what had happened. He said the road was closed and wondered what was happening. He said maybe it was my fault. I started to worry a little," he said. No one is going to know. That night, I never got a wink of sleep, or so it seemed every time I closed my eyes, that noise, the scraping sound, the tires screeching, the massive lorry coming for me. It was a horrible night that seemed like it would never end, but it did, with Mum screaming at me to get out of bed. Everyone else was gone, so I did. She had made tea and toast, but I didn't touch it and returned to bed. When she left. Just before they all came home, Paul came, and we walked. He said am I sick? I was looking pale. Are you scared he said. You had better come and look at this; we went down to the local paper shop, and it read in the small column with a big headline. A 12-YEAR-OLD BOY WANTED; it went on to say. Police are looking for a twelve-year-old boy who's thought to have seen a fatal RTA (road traffic accident) on the main A6666 road police are also looking for. the driver of a red Ford Fiesta and anyone on the A6666. Any information between 9:30 am and 10:30 am may be the missing piece we need, even if you think it is too small. Contact the police on blah blah. I felt sick. It was my fault. Fatal, it had said, someone had died. I lived with this guilt for years and still think about it sometimes. Paul said if I weren't there, it wouldn't have happened. I said if you came out of school, it wouldn't have happened, or at least if you hadn't wanted to go to registration, I wouldn't have been anywhere near that place. He said we could not do anything about it, and we soon went home. We walked to my house as it was on the way to his. We came around the bottom of the road. There was a police car outside my house, Paul and I said at the same time oh shit. He said they had found out. I said I did not want to go home, but I did after arguing with Paul about whose fault it was again. I walked in, and a very nice female policewoman said hi. I said hi, and Mum said you haven't been at school this week, have you? the lady copper then said, "We are going around all the children's houses that weren't at school yesterday from all the schools in the area." is that a lot? I said, "Yes, that's a lot. She said over 110 children just in a 15-mile radius of here". She also said, "We are looking for someone about my age who could have seen an accident near Lutterworth, and did I know anything about that?" she could tell by my face that they had found the right person. She continued, saying I was not in trouble; they wanted to know what I had seen. Dad said if it was you, tell the police what happened. I told them everything, even about Paul playing truant school and the whole registration saga; Dad said so loud it shocked me, "It's him again, always him. I've told you before he is nothing but trouble". It is always the other kid, never your own. With something like this, the policewoman asked whether Paul was with you at the time of the accident. I said no, and the policeman calmed Dad down by saying it's not about why it happened, not yet anyway. We need to know what I had seen; they said they would need to come around tomorrow to take a full statement. Dad said, "Why don't you just do what you should like normal kids, and this would never have happened". thanks, Dad. I felt bad enough to blame myself for this without your help. They had been around Pauls. I found out the next day I thought they would, especially after I had told them everything. Including his address, Paul said they went around, and I was a snitch like I had a choice, I said. Paul said that he walked to school with me because he had missed the bus to school. and had walked because he had been in trouble for not going, always very good at twisting things; he should have come home at lunchtime as he wasn't feeling well. She said did you do that often? No, he told them; his mum said you "had better not! The nice policewoman said that it doesn't matter in this case, but school is important", Paul told me, then she asked if he was walking with me back home, he said no what time did you leave school? just after midday, 'we will call the school.' I was in PE till then, so call and check; they did. He was off the hook.

Chapter 7
Statement

The police came around the next day after I returned from school. I had a bit of hero status. It didn't happen the way I told them in school. Oh no. I said I helped and tried to get one of the people out of the car; I could smell burning; there was blood everywhere, and many kids believed a lot of that, let me tell you. I told the police everything again when they came to take my statement, they asked about what had happened a few days before and why I didn't go to school that week but didn't write much of that down, they started writing when I spoke about the day Though, I told them all about it, even the fact that I was so terrified on the way back after the red car had dropped me off. They asked what was said in the car when I got in and out. (They didn't care how I felt; It could stay with me for life). I said not much, but he said he was going to Leicester, and it looked all under control. And that's why he left; they asked if I had any info on the car, and I said it was an old car and had a dent on the boot, which was great. They said they told me they had a statement from Paul but didn't need anything else. Good, I thought I would tell him this later. What they said next worried me a lot. There will be a court case, and they will need me to tell them everything that happened, the same as what is said here. It would not take long, but you will have someone, a parent or guardian over the age of 21, to accompany you. Maybe

Dad, definitely not; in the end, my sister Mary said she would take me if she could get the time to work. The police said that if I remembered anything else, I could ring them on a number they gave me. Go down the road to the neighbour and say I must phone the police. It's not happening. They did say that if I forgot anything, I would be able to be reminded of my statement, so have I told them everything? I said yes, and I'm sorry. She said that I shouldn't blame myself; things happen, but we must make sure that we try and see if there was any blame, including children going to school. I took a deep breath. She smiled, and I said sorry again. Just do well in school, she said and left.

Chapter 8
Court Case

About three months later, the police came back around. They said there would be a court case, and I might have to give evidence. The guy in the red car did get charged with leaving the scene of an accident. But this was to find out if it was anyone's fault if anyone had caused the death of the two women. I was scared because Andrew had said if they said it was my fault, I wouldn't get out of prison until I was fifty. It would be murder. My oldest sister Mary had to go with me as I wasn't 18. Somebody guided us into a little room; I wasn't in trouble, the man at the court with a big book said. Phew, I thought. He said they're just going to ask you a few questions, and if you can do your best to remember the statement you gave to the police, if you cannot, say, and they will prompt you. But any questions you do answer have to be the truth as you remember them. You are in a court, and lies incur punishment not just for you; the rule is for everyone in this courtroom. I understand, good, he said. Then he asked if we wanted to leave and get some food as somebody would read out the evidence to the court first, and then the court would break for lunch.

Hence, Mary and I went to get some food. The good thing about this was the meal Mary and I had. Mary could claim it back on expenses. It was all a bit spicy for me. It was beginning to return to where it went. But I held it back. We returned to our little room, and at About 2 o'clock, the man came into our little room and said, "They ready for you now. Somebody told me what they would likely ask while waiting, so I wasn't scared. And to be fair, he wasn't that far off. The main reason I was there was this question: when the little red car stopped, did it skid to a stop or very quickly, or did you not even notice how the car had stopped? In your opinion, how do you think the car stopped? I stood up as directed and said, the only thing I noticed about the red car was the front of the car dipped a little; this was nowhere near a skid. And I saw a bump on the boot of the vehicle. It was over twenty minutes, and the questions were all done. We can go," said Mary. I asked who you think was guilty. They told me an open verdict means no one, not even you; she laughed, and I laughed a little. I said, but I thought they said the dog in the cab was the problem. What they said was that the dog had a bearing on the attention of the lorry driver, but the stopping distance of the truck was too much for the time he had to stop; he did the only thing he could do to avoid the child (me) and the red car. Unfortunately, the white car did not have time to take any action, so summing up, I will rule an open verdict; that's what he said. So, what happens now? Mary said the car driver would get some points and a fine for not stopping to help and leaving his name. I think, OK, I said.

Mary was happy she went as she got travel expenses at a day rate for time off work (even though the boss had given her a day off with full pay). She claimed fuel for someone to drop her off at our house the night before, bus fair and both of our meals, even a cup of tea in the café while waiting for the bus. I got home, and they all wanted to know how it went, mainly because they wanted to see if I was in trouble; I wasn't. They left me alone, and I had a cup of tea and a sandwich and went to bed. Ready for school in the morning.

I couldn't wait to tell them all I was a bit of a star. And yes, I had a few stories of what didn't happen, like there was a bit of a fight in the court next to us, one bloke got a punch on the nose, and the guy that hit him got arrested. It never happened; it was just the guy telling someone what would happen, and the person just raised his voice too loud; he soon calmed down when security came, but I had to make it more exciting than that, didn't I? Anyway, I loved life until I started not wanting to Go to school again. One week, something happened every day when I skipped school for six days in a row.

Chapter 9
Week of Woe

Day 1 Monday.

My mate Paul and I were messing about with a football in the house. I was in the kitchen, and he was in the lounge; it was only a light ball; he had to hit the back door through the double doors of the lounge, and I had to hit the wall behind him to get a point. It was getting crazier, kicking the ball harder and harder with each kick, and then, with one massive kick, I got the ball behind him. It didn't hit the wall but broke the window on the bay at the front. The glass wasn't double-glazed; it was a metal framed window with a single thin pane. Panic set in, and I didn't know what to do. I couldn't do anything; I had to wait until Mum got home; she was worried about what Dad would do. Then Andrew came home and started laughing and saying, "Dad's going to kill you. He will throw you out, and you will never come back. Just then, Dad walked in; he wasn't too happy. And shouted a bit, but nothing happened, not this time. Before he could get too mad, I said the front door had slammed when I came in, and it just broke. I just about got away with it. I didn't get a slap, but I didn't get away with being more careful about things that cost money lecture. That went on and on; the longer it went on, the madder Dad became, so we all knew that you must stop talking however you can; luckily, Mum came in and said tea was nearly ready and told me to wash my hands, so off I went smirking.

Day 2 Tuesday.

Again, Paul came around. He was hungry. I was always hungry. Mum had a big sack of potatoes, so I tried to cook some chips in the deep fat frier, a saucepan with a wire mesh basket to hold the chips in. After trying to peel the potatoes and cut them to chip sizes, I put them on the gas ring. Having never cooked anything, I was stirring and stirring them; they turned into what looked like fried mashed potato rather than chips. They were full of fatty oil and probably less healthy than drinking it on its own; anyway, we ate them and then started to mess around again, chasing each other around the house upstairs and down, trying not to fall in the hall.

Behind the front door was a pile of everyone's shoes, and above them were two coat racks with loads of coats that kept falling on the floor. Sometimes, you couldn't open the door fully as there were so many shoes and coats on the floor; it was a solid wooden front door with an arch of four small windows at the top to let some light into the very dark stairs. As soon as you entered the front door, there was a small area where the shoes and fallen coats were. To the left, as you came in, was a door leading into the lounge. About one meter forward was the start of the stairs. So, Paul started throwing shoes upstairs at me, and I would throw them back down at him. He hid around the corner of the wall next to the door frame leading into the lounge and popped out to throw a few up. I hid on the last two steps around the corner to the three-bedroom doors. And I also popped out to throw one down; it was easier for me because I was upstairs. I had not to throw too wild as the shoe would just hit the ceiling and hit the light; one of these shoes continued to go through one of the little windows on the top of the door. Again, I could do nothing to repair it as this was a cut-to-shape window thingy, so I picked up the significant bits of glass, put them back into the hole as best I could, hoping no one would notice and waited. No one noticed until my brother came back. Dam, he doesn't miss much! It may have happened yesterday when the door slammed; I must have cleaned up the glass with the rest of the bay windows. Brilliant, I thought, got away with it. Apart from the normal, it costs even more now lecture. That needed to change, although scary was the same thing repeatedly; Dad must have gotten bored saying it as I was bored of hearing it.

Day 3 Wednesday.

Paul again came around. This time, we just hung out and played a bit of cards. Pontoon was the game we played most with match sticks as pretend money. I soon got bored with that, though, so I decided to play darts. My sister Mary played darts for the county and had an old dart board and proper darts (not the plastic ones; she didn't use those good ones anymore. Above the fireplace was an oval-shaped mirror with plastic trim, trying hard to pretend to be ornate gold, not a chance the cheap-looking thing it was, but Mum liked it. Sometimes in the mornings, Mum lit a fire, nothing like a real fire, to warm a house up. The mirror came down because that was where we hung the dart board. Around the dart board were hundreds of little holes in the big yellow flowery wallpaper that got covered up with the mirror.

Putting the mirror on my Dad's chair out of the way in case of stray darts was intelligent. I was a good darts player and had lots of time to practice so that I would be. I won and won and won again, beating Paul easily. He got fed up with this on the last winning double I threw. He pushed me, and I fell onto my Dad's chair, hearing the sickening sound of the mirror smashing. All on my Dad's cushion and chair. I was horrified we had to mend this sort of thing somehow, but first, we had to get the glass out of my Dad's chair and cushion. I picked up the mirror, and more glass fell onto the floor. After several cuts to my fingers and one on my elbow, I'm not sure how that happened; at least the glass was gone out of the chair, but I got the vacuum cleaner out just in case. Sure enough, some were still there. Paul said good idea of mine to get the vacuum cleaner, yeah and a great idea to push me; after a little row, as usual, I hoped it wouldn't rip the bag in the vacuum cleaner that mum always asked me to put in as it was a little tricky. Now, what do we do about the mirror? In the village, a hardware store sold everything from wood to paint to tools and pots, pans, and every kind of screw and nail you could ever want. And lots more. Besides, I could get the glass on credit; many shops used to give credit.

I was still deciding if we had an account, but I could persuade the shopkeeper to let us have the mirror on credit if they did. I know they sell glass, so hopefully mirrors, too, because that's where Dad went for the bay window glass. We are Saved, I thought. Nope. It had to be machine-cut when I took the mirror frame down. But not having any mirror, I couldn't ask if he would try and have a go at trying to cut it to fit. Dad was angry, and I felt the palm of his hand slap me on the back of my legs. Old shovel hands hurt when he hit you there; just as I was getting over squealing, he gave me one on the back of my head, telling me that I would have to work to pay. Mum was very upset. It didn't matter how many times I said sorry; okay, well, I said it three times, quite a lot for me. I had to work hard to get the next treat, which upset me more than the silent treatment that she gave me. I soon got over it when she found one similar at that weekend's jumble sale at the village hall. Someone's trash is someone else's treasure. I said I would carry it; she said you had better not drop it; that would be the last thing I did. My Dad said I was lucky but still had to work around the house to pay for smashing the horrible dam mirror. The new mirror, to be fair, was a lot nicer, not trying to be a priceless ornate something or other.

Day 4 Thursday.

I went to call around for Paul and hoped his mum wouldn't answer the door. His mum didn't like me much as I was always in trouble with the police, she said. It was funny my Dad didn't like Paul because he said he was always in trouble with the police, but he didn't say it quite like that. His Dad liked me, though, and we used to watch Charles Bronson films at his house and have a go on his drum set sometimes, but his mum was home, so we went back to mine. The fire had been, was still warm, and had dying red embers. After about an hour, it started to get a little cold. There were a few signs of life in the fire, so I looked around for some paper and found some newspaper made balls out of it and threw it on it didn't light, just started to smoke, so I looked around and found a tin of 3 in 1 oil, it had the flame on the side of the can so I knew it was flammable and would help light the fire so I started to squirt on the fire to ignite the embers I didn't notice that the oil went all over the hearth as it was pretty hard to squeeze the tin to make it come out the spout at the top. When I finally got some on the fire, it lit very quickly. The trouble was it burned all the oil on the hearth and the wall on either side of the fireplace. It climbed up the walls on either side of the fireplace, big, angry red and orange flames. Paul and I got scared. I grabbed hold of Mum's mirror. I could not let that get damaged and didn't get burnt. Still, I told Paul to go home; he wanted to anyway, so panicking, I decided to find the number for my sister Joan, who worked at a place everyone called the top factory. It was a knitwear factory at the top of the village. I had found a 10p coin and a couple of 2p coins down the back of my Dad's chair; this was Something I did every day. I often found some change; Paul said let's get some sweets with the money when I saw it. We used to buy fruit salad and black jacks; chewy sweets were my favourite 3 for 1p bargain, but I needed it now the red BT phone box at the bottom of our road used to take 2p and 10p coins I was not going to go around our neighbours and tell them that I think I've set the house on fire in the Phone box you could press 0 and make a reverse charge call through the operator if you didn't have any coins, but this was a factory, and the receptionist wouldn't have taken the cost, when asked by the operator, so I called and told her that I needed to speak to my sister urgently, it seemed to take Joan ages to get her on the other end of the phone so long in fact that the pips sounded as soon as she said hello, the pips told you your money had ran out and you only had a few seconds to put more money in before the call was ended, so as she answered I shouted down the phone I've set the lounge on fire a load of flames went up the side of the fire place I only put some newspaper on the fire and flames were everywhere. She said she was coming and she would call the fire brigade. I went home expecting to see the house on fire, but it wasn't. I went into the lounge, and the fire was out, but there were some black scorched Pauls where the flames went up the side of the fireplace and onto the ceiling. Joan came bursting into the room out of breath as she had run from the top factory a distance that was. She was shouting what have you done? Looking around, she calmed down and quickly gasped at the state of the wall around the fireplace. The fire had hardly touched the wooden fire surround; somebody told me later that the fire would only burn while there was oil to burn, and nothing caught fire. As soon as all the oil burnt away, the flames would have stopped but left a mark on the wall. Joan angrily said I must clean that mess up before Dad comes home. The fire brigade arrived, lights going, and sirens and people in the street came out to look; Joan had to tell them it was a false alarm. One came in to have a look and very sternly said to her that. She then returned to work, probably cursing me all the way home. I used washing-up liquid mainly, but even though most came off, you could still see the damage to the wallpaper around the fireplace. I had ruined it. As you can imagine, Dad was unhappy and told me in no uncertain terms how his son could be so stupid. Harsh, I thought. But the clip around the ear now was standard. We had to change the wallpaper eventually and changed it to an ensemble that was even worse; you cannot imagine how bad this wallpaper was; it was a flock (raised pattern) not quite matching the join's flowers and trees and some other things maybe clouds not only that, got painted with the worst purple colour yes Purple it was awful, the amount of teasing I got from my siblings never ended the night of the fire night. It continued through the next few days, like when someone said turn something on or up. "don't let me do it. I will turn it up too much. "Ha bloody Ha, but there were other problems to come through,

Day 5 Friday.

It was the week from hell for Mum and Dad. and it was only Friday. We wanted to stay in the house but got bored, so we went to the park and played on the swings, seeing how high we could go. Paul was always better at stuff like that than me, as I had more self-preservation than he did. He didn't care so much about getting hurt. Again, Paul and I got bored and returned to my house and found Andrew's video card for the shop next to the top factory that used to hire videos out. The guy who ran it didn't care that we were young and we often got naughty videos. Saying it was for my brother. I am trying to remember where we got the money or if it was on account. We found a key that looked like a key to my Dad's car that was in the garage; my Dad had gone to work in his van, so we thought we could go up in the car because Paul could drive, not legally, we had been to the banger racing for Pauls, an older friend we for some reason looked up too. he sometimes let us move the car around Paul mostly, I had a go, but as per usual I was scared, he loved it he had to drive before the race began, every time would ask if one day Drive in the race, his mate said you can, one day, maybe. That was it; he never got to do it. After the final race, you could not drive any of the cars. They called it banger racing; indeed, they were bangers. It took ages to get the car started and turn the key in the ignition. At last, it started. Paul had to reverse out of the garage. He caught one of the mirrors, but it didn't do any damage. I put it back in its correct position. Off we went, driving past the high school that I should have been at. The V sign went up. We laughed, but soon, it wouldn't be all fun and games. We got to the shop, and he turned off the car. We got out and picked our film, confessions of something or other confessions of a window cleaner; I think, quite a lot of nudity but not porn. The problems started here. We went out all smug because we got the film and got into the car. Still, it wouldn't start. We tried for ages and ages. He had a go. I had a try, then him, me again, panicking more and more. We had ruined my Dad's ignition, and the factory where my sister Joan worked was nearly coming out for break time. We did not know if my sister would come to the shop to get anything, so we ran home, leaving the car, avoiding going past the school I should have been in; we knew all about the jitty's as we called them a little path joining one road to another not wide enough for a car, but wide enough for a moped especially when being chased by the police, These would come in handy when we had motorbikes. We knew a bike could get through all the little paths and dead ends, but not a car. After a while, we got home. I didn't know what to do but came up with a plan that seemed perfect in my head. Dad was working in a village about 5 miles away; I always tried to find out where Dad was working, asking if he had built the wall. I said it like I wanted to learn how to do these things. I learned how to do loads of things, and to do them correctly, I started working with Dad. I didn't get a lot but earned a little wage. I would join him and Andrew after leaving school. But I wanted to know if there was a chance he would come home early, so that's why I would ask all the questions; there was always that chance he would pop back to get some tools he forgot; the van was parked on the front all the time when Dad came home, and that gave us enough time to hide. Or I would say that I was ill or had a study day or some bullshit while Paul hid under my bed. He did not like Paul, so I dreaded what would have happened if he had found him; it was bad enough when he would call around for me. I thought of a plan to get on my bike and tell Dad I needed the house keys as I had locked myself out. With the excuse of getting my sports kit for the afternoon PE lesson, I did this for a gamble, but I knew that his car key was on his one bunch with his van and house keys. He moaned a bit about me being more responsible. While I was there, I could mix another batch of mortar as he was building a wall, so after mixing it and after, he moaned a little because it was too sloppy. He would have to put more sand and cement in, so it was not much of a time saver that he should have done it himself (yes, I thought you should have). He then shocked me and said, you're not in trouble again, are you? I gulped and said no. Apart from being late for PE. He told me that the keys were in his bag and for me to leave the van key; brilliant, I thought. I got Dad's car key and nearly dropped the whole bunch a few times on the way home because I was rushing; imagine them falling out of my hand and into a drain; that would have been it. I Rode back home and had another thought: why didn't we go to the shop on the bike? I suppose I wouldn't have gone on my own; he wouldn't have been able to get the film with my brother's membership card, and he wouldn't croggy me all the way there, not far but far enough, then Paul and I walked to get the car Brake time was over so Joan wouldn't be around, I hoped. Feeling smug, I got in the car and tried the key, but it wouldn't go in. I had to force it a little and tried turning, but it wouldn't even turn. We had broken the barrel. Panicking, I tried to push it more and more in and out, trying harder and harder to make it turn. Then it did turn, but that was because the key had snapped in the barrel. Shit, no, what am I going to do now? I felt like crying; I did a bit, I think. A big lump came into my throat I couldn't swallow for ages; in a small voice, I said I'm dead now. We walked back home straight past the school and didn't care. Now, we'll probably not be alive after Dad discovers what happened. The time it took from me getting home to Dad coming home was ages that seemed like years. The ticking from the cheap-looking gold carriage clock with a glass dome and three ball shapes going around at the bottom, sitting on top of the TV, sounded like a church bell inside my head. I won't lie; I was shitting myself, Dad pulled up. I went cold, nearly passing out; the words that I had prepared to tell him went straight out of my head; I couldn't breathe, let alone talk. He always put his best tools into the garage; oh no, he's going to find out. I couldn't do anything; I wanted to run. I tried to hide but couldn't, and the tears rolled down my face. They got wiped away, and out I go to face the thunder that is my Dad. I didn't want it all to happen inside so the little darlings my siblings could watch; as I went out the back door, he came out of the garage with eyes as dark as the night sky at midnight. He grabbed me and screamed where is the car, you little bastard? What have you done with my car? One of his massive hands was around my throat. It went almost three-quarters of the way around, squeezing the life out of me. I screamed, but the noise that came out was a whimper. He released his grip slightly. I said it's at the shop. It broke down. He let me go, grabbed my arm, and dragged me into the house. My mum was there, shouting, asking what was going on and what had happened. Dad loosened his grip. I got away and tried to run past Andrew but didn't quite make it. He did enough to get in my way for Dad to catch me. He soon grabbed me, threw me onto the sofa, and shouted tell me what you have done. Tell me where my car is! Then Joan came in and heard this and said that his car was at the top shop near where she works as she had wondered what it was doing there. Dad heard and turned his oh-so-scary eyes back on me, burning into the very part of me that couldn't lie for fear of more suffering. I wanted to disappear, so you wanted the keys, you little bastard. He said with exasperation. I was holding back the tears not only from the pain in my throat but also because my arm was starting to throb. The tears were on their way because of the absolute fear coursing through my body like the wind rushing past you when you stand on the top of a mountain. I spoke in a frail voice. I'm sorry I broke the key in the car ignition. I'm sorry, I'm sorry, I kept saying even after he got up and gave me a slap across my face that would leave a mark for a day, then a bruise for a few days more, Andrew, Joan and worse of all the want to be nurse Julie came home. And the questions came, I couldn't say anything. I got the ribbing; I got the pain, the hurtful words, and the feeling of being rubbish was more substantial that day than ever. After Dad slapped my face and the rest of them had their say, I went upstairs and sobbed, feeling sorry for myself for wanting to die, and that would show them, but I wasn't that selfish or Brave. Dad went down the road and asked Ken, a neighbour, to see if he could help get his car back. He and Dad went up to the vehicle in Dad's van and, after about 2 hours, came back. Ken was driving the car. Dad was driving the van; I found out from my lovely siblings I couldn't go anywhere near Dad, let alone ask him anything about the. They said Ken had to break off the ignition and jump-start the car to get it back. It would cost loads to get a new one fitted, and if they lost out on anything, I would pay a lot. Great, I thought it just goes on and on.

Day 6 Saturday.

I thought it was all over. I wanted it to be all over, but it wasn't. On Saturday morning, Andrew had a bonfire; I am not sure what he was burning, but the neighbours two doors down had one. Andrew said go and get some paper from the shed. The blue wooden shed was full of newspaper; I had no idea why, but the wooden floor had so much paper. You couldn't even see it. We never really kept anything else in there, the odd wooden bench and a few old tools; most of the garden stuff was in the other shed, the better one without the rubbish in it. We made that fire big. It smouldered all afternoon much better than the neighbours. Dad said before going to the bingo, poor water on it to make sure it was out. So Andrew did; I loved it. I could not believe how much heat came from that thing. I stayed out most of the afternoon poking and adding sticks and hearing it crackle. I put an old bike tyre on it, and the smoke turned black. Then somebody shouted from the kitchen window and told me to leave it alone. Mum and Dad went off to bingo. Julie said, did I want a game of table tennis? We didn't have a proper table tennis table; we used our kitchen table and had a net that you hooked on either side in the middle; it worked fine. While Julie was setting it up, I went outside to see the fire. It was dark, and there was no sign that it was still alight. But I noticed that Andrew had left the matches on the bin. So, I went to the Blue shed and lit some paper under the door. Just then, Julie shouted, are you ready, so I put my foot on the flame that was trying so hard to keep lit. After a few stomps on the flame, I went inside to play table tennis; our back door had a small square frosted window that let some light in, but you couldn't see through it. The kitchen was always dark. After 10 minutes, Julie noticed an orange glow through the kitchen window and said what's that? I don't know. I said, come on, you serve. Hang on and open the door. She screamed, FIRE, FIRE! Andrew came running. Tim started barking. The neighbours came running, Not the neighbours with the fire but those on either side of us, probably worried that it might spread to them. The one with the phone had already rung the fire brigade. The blue shed was at the top of the garden under a holly tree. Even though there is a lot of green on them, green trees don't burn quickly, but that tree was very badly burnt, as were the trees close to it. The fire brigade was only a few minutes; it seemed like hours. Everyone was getting buckets of water and hose pipes and trying to keep the fence and the trees wet, but it didn't help much. The fire brigade parked outside and ran a hose to the back garden; they asked Andrew what could blow up in the shed. Andrew said paper and maybe some old paint. They soon put the fire out. Then the questions came. Who was the adult? Luckily, Dawn had returned before the fire brigade and said she was in charge. She asked us the same questions as the fire brigade was asking. I said I didn't know anything about it; I was playing table tennis with Julie, and they asked about the fire we had earlier, but Andrew said that Dad had told him to pour water over it. Wise, the fireman said. How did this happen? I wonder, looking at me. I said as quick as a flash. The neighbours had a fire earlier; maybe a spark came from there. Mum and Dad came home about then. And he was shouting at everyone, demanding to know what was happening. The fireman said we can only be sure once we speak to the neighbours. Why do you need to talk to them? Dad said. Because you were not the only one to have a fire today, my Dad said, I would have a word. No, the fireman said, we will come back to you. They went around and got a statement from them. The fireman returned and said it was possible that a spark from yours, or theirs, might have gotten into the shed and was very unlucky to have started the fire. Still, with all that paper in there, it was an accident waiting to happen. Dad went quiet. They left, and so did Dad, to go to the neighbours. Mum told me to go to bed. It was 25 years before they knew the truth; they always blamed the neighbours. From then on, I kept out of Dad's way for a few weeks. I knew being in the same room would be dangerous, so I went out before he came home and returned after he went to bed, climbing in the bedroom window if I was locked out.

Chapter 10
Park

Paul and I went for a walk in the park. We used to go to this park a lot. All it had was a seesaw and a set of three swings for us older kids, and three swings with a highchair look about them. For the younger kids, we did, on occasion, try to get into the baby swings. Let me tell you, it was easier to get in than to get out. There was a very long slide, not very steep. It was on a hill, no wait, more of a slope that was more fun running up the side than sliding down part. There was a cricket pitch, a poorly kept football pitch, and a Pavilion, nothing worth getting in there for. A small mound of earth separated the cricket pitch and the football pitch. And another Separated them from the rest of the park. The park was boring, even though the birdcage was always a challenge. It was a series of pipes about a meter long in squares to climb through up, down, right and left. just a load of metal squares, one on top of another, looked like something that should not have been in a children's park. It was more suited to an army assault course. It was massive; it had eight squares long, eight squares up, and eight squares deep, all the holes being a meter square. We used to race to the top, to the back, and then to the floor. The trick was not to fall off; you could fall off anywhere, and nothing could stop you from falling through the bars; let me say you knew it. If you did, even if you didn't hit the solid pipes on the way down, it was concrete waiting for you and not grass at the bottom. Many casualties because of that thing. That was always fun for an hour or two. One time, we had a game called Cat and Mouse. You had to start at the middle at the top and get down onto the floor before being tagged. The other person had to run around and get you before you got a foot on the floor. Your foot had to be outside of the bars. Still, you could put your foot down on the bottom level to help hop over the bottom set of bars; you could always crouch down and try and run under the bars to get out of the frame, but that mostly ended with a concussion, I had seen stars more than once, trying that trick. It was a good game, easy for the person on the outside, though most times that wasn't me; we used to invent games like who could throw darts off the top of the bars furthest. I had a good arm, and so did Paul, so this was always quite close; we did it with stones, but Paul used to say that mine was better, lighter, or rounder. He never liked losing. I didn't do much either, but I never made a song and dance about not winning, not out loud anyway, so we used darts. We could see how far we had thrown them and put something down to mark where it landed our jumper or coat. Like we used to do when we played football, to make a goal, there were no proper goalposts, only the ones they would put up when there was a game on, and sometimes not take down. But the little darlings (kids) would climb all over them, and one kid fell off the top and broke his arm; another cut his hand badly on the hooks that used to hold the nets onto the crossbar. So, after that, we had to use coats. So, Paul threw the three darts. We occasionally used Mary's darts but got caught because we never cleaned them. She had seen it when she came around for a bingo game one weekend. I said you don't want them, or you would take them home, she said, I don't mind anyone playing with them as they are my spare set, but with a dart board, not throwing them all around the garden. This one day, though I was on the floor ready to get them for my throw, Paul threw the two. We argued about where I put the shirt. He said it was further back; I moved it a little as he threw the last dart. I looked around for where it landed, and he started laughing so much that he nearly fell off the bars. I shouted where did it go, he laughed more and called back, look up! I looked up, and he started laughing again; all I could see were clouds; he pointed to his head, and I shouted yeah, you are bonkers. "No, he said, still laughing, it is in your head. The dart was in my skull just above my ear; I never felt a thing. I didn't even know it had hit me, alone stuck in my head. I reached for it, pulled it out, and continued with the games for a few more goes each. The seesaw didn't get left out. We always tried to hurt one another on that by pushing up as hard as we could to make the other one hit the floor hard with both feet. And that sometimes hurt more than a lot. Everyone used to do this. I think.

Chapter 11
Brother

My Dad did not deserve the things I did to him, let alone all the trouble Andrew got into when he was a teenager. He wasn't horrible, not a bully; he was to me, like when we played in the garden, chasing each other. I was quick, and he couldn't catch me easily. This one time he did, he pushed me; I was running towards the back door, trying to get into the house before he got me. But all the push did was send me flying; the trouble was I was close to the kitchen window, and the next thing I knew, I was on the floor with blood streaming down my face. Judy screamed and ran into the house, shouting Mum! I had only smashed my head on the house bricks that sat in a square around the drain. To stop leaves and things going into the drain to block it. I lifted my hand to my forehead and felt a deep cut on my brow between my eyebrows above my nose. Mum came out and screamed at Andrew because he was laughing. Mum told him to go to the house. As he went, he said it might knock some sense into me and laughed again. He was the class clown who would find things funny for him but not for anyone else. Sometimes comedy can be hurtful, like when he got a hold of Dawn's Diary. She wrote everything down in her diary. I never bothered to find it and have a read. I probably wouldn't like what I saw anyway. Still, she did on occasions read out some stuff that she had written, like the thing about "I did a great painting in school today, a picture of my time at the park." the teacher, Mrs Brockleston, "said that she thinks it is the best work I had done this term", (made me very happy), so there was never enough juicy stuff in it for me. Although Andrew did find some once, it was the stuff of legends, all about this boy David and how she would hold him all through the night, and even let him put his hands under her clothes and that she bet he was a perfect kisser. One passage read that she had a very naughty dream about the naughty things he was doing to her, and in the morning, she was hot and wet; Andrew loved this. I didn't know much about this and what it meant. Still, I did taunt her with it by putting my hand up my shirt and moving it around and making all kinds of moaning noises, saying oh David, David, oh David, she was so hurt and cried so much that she almost made me feel guilty Almost, Andrew with his best mate from next door, David. It was more than a match for what Paul and I would get up to one time at the park. Those two were messing about on the seesaw as we all did, but David would sometimes go too far; they would try and push up hard so the other would hit the bottom hard and hurt your bum; we did this also. But David put his legs down and locked his knees just after Andrew had pushed up with all his power because the seesaw stopped going up; Andrew did not and went over the top onto his back, still holding onto the little handle that made you feel somewhat safe. And bit almost through his tongue. Now, our doctor at the time was a very strange old man who looked like he had given up on life years ago but was somehow committed to being a doctor until the day he died, which he did. So, as they say, you must take your hat off to him. But as Andrew found out he did some strange things in the name of medicine, I found out later how he stopped the blood. He did it by putting a load of cotton wool in his mouth, and to this day, Andrew cannot touch cotton wool, even finding it hard to pull wire wool apart. Later, I would have bugged him with cotton wool when I could. He had to go to the hospital for stitches on his tongue. Oh yes, that is going to hurt. Not as much as the time Andrew got a piece of metal in his eye and was cutting his eye. It was a severe problem, but I had to give him some. Hey, you are going to go blind. I said it serves you right, he tried to slap me but missed as he could not see correctly. Mum took him straight down to Dr Burnes. He, and his incredible ways, got a syringe and poked around Andrew's eye until he reached the bit of metal and got it out of his eye. Badly scratched and very painful. He had put a bandage over his eye, but it was before the seesaw thing; it would have been interesting if it were after. The doctor told Mum he would live. He was fortunate that the bit of metal went to the bottom of his eye socket, which made it easier to get out; if it had come loose, he would have lost his sight in that eye, but he would be able to see out of it soon. Andrew had tears in his eyes. I said have you been crying? You cry, baby, and this time, his slap did catch me even though he looked like a weird pirate. I went to the lounge, and he went upstairs and was asleep when I got to bed later. It wasn't the best idea to do what the doctor did, but it worked. He probably saved his sight in that eye, but when he showed it to me, the eyeball was a weird shade of yellow, but his sight came back perfectly. The cops used to come around a lot when I was very young; one time, he smashed a load of windows and had to go to court. He got a fine and struggled to pay it off; I don't think he learned his lesson from that because my Dad once had to pick him up from the train station. Dad told him to start walking and would meet him halfway, which was his way of punishing him, I think. I went with Dad to see what Dad would say, and I hoped he would have a go at Andrew; when we got to him, Andrew told us what had happened. He and David were at the seaside and had set a rubbish bin on fire when they were drunk. Andrew, who also had a mean streak, told me that when the cops put him in a jail cell for the night to appear in court the next day on a criminal damage charge, the cops started to ruff him up. They did that sort of thing then. Teenagers are always a problem for the police. Andrew, my Hero now, said they were forcing him into the cell, and he was fighting back. He said as they threw him into the cell with a copper on each arm and one on a leg; he said to me that he shouted, "One of you pig bastards will have to leave last." He went up in my hero ladder after that. Dad, on the other hand, smacked him on his nose with the back of his hand and started his nose bleeding. He said you can walk again if you use language like that in my car. Sorry, he said in a weak voice. His being a hero from then on was fading fast. He seemed weak, but most people next to Dad were weak. Andrew and his mate David had a thing for fires and started a few in tinder-dry fields for no reason. I am not sure if it was him, but someone Had set the field behind the petrol station on fire. And it got seriously close to the petrol station. It was so bad that they had four fire engines there to try and stop the fire. And evacuated half the street around the petrol station, pretty much everyone was watching. Some hoped it would all go up in a massive, big bang. The firefighters kept pushing us back, so Paul and I went around the top field to watch from a bit of a hill. It was a brilliant view; I could see everything: the two ambulances, the four cop cars, the firefighters running around like blue-arsed flies, and maybe a film crew from the local news channel, but more like a photographer. It never got to the petrol station, making the local news on TV and in the paper. We tried to see if we were in the film, but we weren't recognised because we moved around to try and get the best view. A few said they had seen one of the brothers grim. We said at the same time again they would be in if they fell in. The police came around to interview him. The three policemen then went looking for David next door after they had finished with Andrew; they couldn't find him. He was hiding under his mum's bed, and his mum said he was out. She nearly got taken away for lying to the police, but nothing came of it. The police could not prove it was them, and they never confessed to it. Dad would not allow anyone to lie to the police, so Mum could never do that for us, even if she wanted to. Andrew teased me because of my sticky-out ears, so he made a name for me: WAFF. He never called me Steve after that; if he did need to use a name, he would only use WAFF. He said it was because I kept wafting the air with my big ears. It's funny how some names can hurt, and some don't, but every time I heard that, it was like someone sticking a pin into me. He and Juile could be so mean we would all be playing with balloons filled with air, and you couldn't let it hit the floor, or you lost a point; you could only hit it, you couldn't catch it. I liked this game; I was quick and good at hitting it back; you should never hit it too hard, and I had two hits to get it back to their side. If you hit it too hard, it would spiral and not go straight. That was great; what wasn't so great was they always had to burst balloons behind my head. I was always so into the game that I was never ready for the big bang behind me. Even now, I hate when a balloon pops, especially if it is behind me. Other load bangs don't affect me like that balloon bang, apart from the odd cork coming out of a bottle that gets me if it is behind me sometimes. They used to say horrible things and make me cry a lot when I was young. I still remember the absolute fear that I felt when they used to say. WATCH OUT; THERE IS A

GREEN HAND COMING OUT OF THE WALL. It's coming to get you; don't look; if you look, it will get you and carry you away. I was so scared I could not lift my head; they then changed where it was and said it was coming from the TV or the sofa. I was petrified; all I could do was cry, but they kept on and on, and I would scream and sob or run away and hide upstairs in bed under the blankets. Like that will save me, that stopped when they found love. Andrew had only met a girl called Karren. She lived in a village about 8 miles away. The only way he could get there was on the bus. I remember him using blue ink from a pen and a needle to tattoo the letter K on his arm; not long after that, they fell out, and he changed it to an anchor shape. I got a lot of slaps for taking the mick out of him while he did that, followed by a stick of the pin. Julie found love with a boy called George in the village where we used to go to the bingo. So, Dad used to drop her off on the way and pick her up on the way back. Until they split up, he was horrible to Julie, and Dad wanted to go and give him a slap or two. But Julie said he wasn't worth it; she soon found another man and was happy. Happy days.

Chapter 12
Hurt

Dad had enough to worry about without me coming along and stepping into the shoes that Andrew had now vacated, starting to conform to what he was. It had to be the arrival of girls in his life, and the fact David, his best mate, had gone away probably to jail was a blessing. But Andrew had a problem gambling with bandits, which was his thing. These had a jackpot of £5, quite a lot. Well, it used to be five goes for 50 pence. I also got hooked but didn't know it then, but I would soon know when I started earning my own money. I used to watch Mum play them at the club. The jackpot was £50. Mum never won the jackpot but got a couple of £10. I loved her winning as I would get something from the bar or go to school the next morning. If Mum had stopped playing because she didn't win. There was an old lady, and her name was Ida. I also used to watch her, and she would make me laugh about the symbols on the machine saying juicy Lucy lemons all in a row for me. She would say I brought her luck if she won and often got me some sweets in her bag, but I would only get them if we won; it wasn't that often, but when she did, I won with chewy sweats. I used to wait for Andrew to finish work on a Thursday night and get off the bus, and he would go into the pub and play on the machine. I used to watch him instead; I was obsessed with them. It was in the pub's ally where they played long ally skittles. that was a weird game. It was like bowling but had nine wooden pins and a wooden chute where to put the ball thing in to roll back to the end you threw them from. I would say that the ball was not a ball. It was more like a big fat rolling pin half the length but 20 times the thickness, and if it popped out of the shoot, well, more like a trough, higher one-end gravity would help it get back to the throwing line. It was a weird game on its way back because it never rolled properly; the ball cheese or whatever they called it wouldn't roll straight and sometimes would bounce and hit random stuff or people if they weren't watching. Dad had been made redundant from his maintenance job at a big industrial Centre, a Job for life there. They said most of my siblings worked there at one time or another; even Mum worked as a cleaner there for a while. That's where Andrew was still working as a painter, painting the insides of massive oil drums, he said. Dad's redundancy was a shock to us all. He had to leave because he had a slight problem with Vertigo. When Dad went up a ladder one time, he went dizzy, and the Doctor said it was fine, but he couldn't rule out the fact that it may happen again. Dad then had to work for a builder in a small village about three miles away; he knew him from when he worked with him after doing his 5-year apprenticeship in bricklaying. He had started his own building business with his two sons and was doing well. He knew Dad and respected him in and around our village, and together, they built some of the houses on the main road in the village. so they knew each other well. Dad worked for him for cash and would have an envelope of cash every weekend. it was too tempting for me; around then, Paul had just stolen a car again but had to ditch it. He had hit the Curb and popped one of the tires. Going too fast around a corner and nearly losing control of the car slowed him down a bit; one time, when I was skipping school, I searched for money and went into Mum and Dad's room. Most times, there were a few coins on the side, or that had rolled under the bed. I'm out of Dad's trousers, but today, JACKPOT! two, yes, two envelopes with notes in my God, I had never seen as much money as that. I went downstairs and tried to think of a way of having some, but I knew if I did, it would be curtains for me. I couldn't help it. I helped myself to one envelope with nearly £100 in it. I ran to Paul's house and told him what I had found and never told him about the other envelope, but he said let's go to the coast there's a party pub there with loads of women. I said I have got to put it back. Dad will kill me. As we debated this, walking down the road, we saw the car for sale, no mot or tax, £55, a sign. Paul said let's do it, let's buy it; we can go to the party in it. He said we would get the girls; they love blokes with cars. I believed him. We got it for £50. I said it was for my brother, and if he gave us the keys, he would come and get it later. Then, I said he would work anyway, and we had paid, so it was ours. so we had the keys. We had a car, and we sure would get some girls now. We returned to my house, and I did one of the things I regret most. Out of all the things I did to my dad. I wrote a note for my dad on the plastic ornate mirror above the fireplace, saying I don't want to be a part of this family anymore. I have taken an envelope, and Dad can call it my inheritance; we can call it quits, and in big letters, I wrote BYE! One word did more than I ever thought it would do. It ripped Mum apart, and I found out later that Dad was upset, too. He didn't speak, was quiet for ages, and wouldn't talk to anyone, just a huh or hey or yep. Sorry, Dad, if you're seeing this wherever you are. We went to the coast, spent it all, never got a girl, and brought a few girls a drink or two. I didn't know it then, but we got taken for a ride. They disappeared at the end of the night as the money did, and to top it off, the car broke down on the way back. the money did. I abandoned the car, so I had to thumb a lift home. It took two days, and we slept in a barn overnight.

Chapter 13
Animals

I am the youngest of six, good in some ways and bad in lots more ways. My siblings saw me as a spoiled brat, and that was mostly true. But I was a good manipulator, especially with Mum and Dad. On the other hand, it was not as easy. He would be in the room, and most of the fun had to stop. He always said, "Kids should be seen and not heard." he didn't mean it, but if we were too loud, you would soon know it with just a look or a word; normally, hey, shut up. He never called us by our names like Julie, shut up, just hey or a noise like a sigh and a look. But if that look changed, and he switched from annoyed to angry, you left, do not stay around. It was not so bad for the others, or so it seemed, as I was always the one that got it in the neck, back in those early memories of mine. They would say I got away with so much if you asked them, but I was always in trouble. I remember a wild black cat coming into our coal house every year. The coal house was what it sounded like; it was a home for coal. We no longer had coal; the cat would have her kittens yearly. Not all of them survived. Sadly, we had to bury them in the ditch at the top of the garden, like a pet cemetery up there. (Every year, she would return, but we, mostly Julie, would look after them. There are many images in my mind, mostly of a small syringe with milk in feeding them kittens; she mostly did a good job. I thought I was young and helped as best I could, but I lost interest after a week or so. One day, Julie and I were feeding the kittens. In the lounge, Tim, the dog, was told to lie down, and after a good sniff and an odd bark that scared the kittens, he did and left us alone, so there we were feeding the kittens. Dad came in, unsure where we were normally good at knowing when he was coming, but not today; he saw us with them and shouted to get them mangey things out. Dad didn't like them. I think he thought they had fleas, more like he thought it would cost him money as Tim did for dog food, but Dad liked dogs' cats didn't do anything apart from crap on your lawn. I wasn't going to tell him that dogs do too. Dad wouldn't pay vets' bills. I found out later. Tim was a special dog to me, a collie sheepdog mix. He used to dig holes, put his nose in it, blow out, dig a bit more, sniff, blow out through his nose and dig again, but he never found anything. I felt safe taking him for walks even if I saw the brothers grim. They would avoid us; Tim wouldn't have done anything, but thank God they never knew that. But one of the worst things ever was finding out that he had a form of skin disease on his back, lost most of his hair, was scabby and didn't look great. The others used to say keep away from him as I would catch what he had. And all my hair will fall out. I didn't care. He used to come and lie with me when I was on the floor, watching TV, and we would cuddle up so very nicely; they could all get lost if they thought I was ever going turn my back on my Tim, even though he was getting sicker and sicker hardly wanting to play just wanted to lie down. One day, Mum, Andrew and I had to take Tim to the vet. it is where we found out that it was a disease on his back, and it would slowly drive him insane with the heat of the summer coming up. Dam that sun, the vet said that "it would be costly to treat." No, no, I thought, don't talk about money. And I'm not listening to you. "It was very cruel to make him go through it, even with the treatment. I tried not to listen, but I heard I cried floods and floods of tears, crying so much I couldn't breathe. money, why was it always about money? Tim, I heard myself shout, I won't let them I won't, he was in the other room. I could see him through the glass. He heard my voice, stood up, looked at me straight into my eyes, lay down one more glance at me, and closed his eyes. noooo! I screamed as loud as I could; I was then ushered and dragged outside, still panting with the tears rolling down my face and the noise coming out of my mouth like a full-on thunderstorm with all the rain, tears and noises that came with it. If I had a gun, I swear, at that moment, I would have shot the vet to stop him from killing my Tim. Mum went in to talk to the vet. I wanted to go with her, But Andrew would not let go of me. I tried to get lost but couldn't; we both knew what that meant. Andrew tried to help me in my distressed state and tried to make it better by saying it was best for him. He was in pain and had been for a long time, and I was selfish to want to take him home to suffer. Why did it seem like he blamed me? I would hold him to make him better. He went for a walk with me last week. I was making him better, I sobbingly said. Don't be stupid, he said he's gone, He won't be coming back, come on and started to walk away. Let Mum deal with it. I couldn't. I ran back to the vet and nearly got hit by a car. it didn't matter; nothing could hurt me. Nothing would stop me from saving Tim. just as Mum returned to the waiting room. All I could see was the lead. Tim's lead. No, I heard myself shout, please no. Tim, no, Tim, don't go, come back. It's time for your walk; come on, boy. He wasn't going to come. The only thing left was just his lead with the half-chewed brown leather handle leading down to a silver clip that was still clipped onto the metal chain with two large rings at the end, so if Tim got too excited, you would give a sharp pull, and that would pretty much strangle him then loosen again, he was very excited always wanting to be leader, well until this last year. I couldn't cope. I screamed something murderer or something like that, snatched the lead, and ran all the way home sobbing so much I couldn't see very well where I was going. I ran past Andrew at the black pad, as we called the path linking the top of our road to the main road where that dam vet was. I pushed him; he shouted something. I could not hear him. My heart was going to burst with pain. this pain I will never forget. Never forget. I still have Tim's lead with me somewhere. Dad, I said we were only trying to feed them; Dad came over to take them off us both. Julie quickly got up and passed me in front of Dad, slowing him down; he slowed enough for me to get up and turn my back. And walk towards the back door to put them back into the coal house where their Mum was meowing, a strange noise, not a normal meow, more like a cat screaming, probably because we had her kittens. She would never come into the house. She was scared. We put the kittens back in the cardboard box we got from the coop on top of an old cushion; it didn't matter what cushion. They were all old. But the cats loved it. It was a perfect place for them. The coal house was the old place where the coalman would put the coal after carrying it on his shoulder. He was so dirty with all the coal flakes all over him, though he stopped coming a while ago; there wasn't any coal in there now, just a load of rubbish as we must have gone to the central heating. Some people had coal bunkers, large concrete boxes with a hole on the top and sliding hatches at the front to get the coal out. The door house had a brick shed type thing with a door on the front split down the middle with a brick wall, half on their side and half on ours; our house, as most semi-detached houses built then, were the same they joined like this down the middle, a mirror image if you put a line from front to back the house the coal house even the size and layout of the garden was identical. The coal house was only big enough for two bikes but had a full-sized door. It had one large concrete flat roof, shared between the two, where we would sunbathe sometimes, as you couldn't get water thrown up there. It never stopped me trying, though; the cat stopped screeching and began to lick the kittens. It looked like she would lick their fur off them; she must be trying to get the smell of humans out of her babies. I watched as she and the kittens cuddled up, and it seemed like they would fall asleep anyway. By then, I had lost interest and started returning to the lounge. Dad had gone to bed for the afternoon, so it must have been a weekend. Mum was washing as per normal. I sometimes helped her; you had to be careful though the way that mixer thing went round, well half way round one way and halfway around the other way as quick as a flash it could catch you unawares and try and grab your hand a pull it, that's why we had a heavy poker to poke the clothes under the water, the other part of the twin tub was a spinner, the dam thing would go so fast the whole washing machine tried to walk across the kitchen floor, that's if the dam thing didn't leak first, many a time we have had to put that pipe on that went into the kitchen sink and mop up the smelly water of the floor. I liked to help hold the lid down on the spinner as that popped open sometimes and stopped it spinning, sitting on it sometimes. But the best thing was that we had a mangle to use after the spinner had finished. It was a dangerous thing and should not be allowed anywhere other than a torture chamber, as a few times I was. It had one solid wooden bar above another with a big cog and a handle on the side; the wooden bars were very close together, so as you turned, it pulled the clothes through and pressed them half to death, and got rid of the excess water, onto a shoot and back into the washing machine, they were dry enough to hang on the airer but still dripped a bit so if possible we would put them outside on the washing line if not out came the pots and pans to catch the water. One day, not so long after this, the mother cat brought a kitten into the kitchen, dropped it, and went around the kitchen, into the lounge, and finally behind the sofa. There she died; the last thing she could do was come into the house that always protected her babies and made sure we knew they needed us again by dropping one in the kitchen. We watched as she found a cool, dark place to finish her days and probably very long nights; she did so well as there were foxes around. One of them ate one of our rabbits now. I was very young and easily fooled sometimes, and Julie had said that the foxes had gotten him. He had gotten out of his cage. He left the cage a lot and ate whatever he could find in the garden. some mornings, I had to try to catch him before school; I was not surprised he got eaten by the fox; that thing was older than me and probably wasn't a fast runner anymore. and now he was the fox's dinner. for years, I feared foxes. I had never seen one at that point, and when I did, I was a bit nervous, but Tim was around, and he would have saved me. I am sure the fox did not stay around to find lovely-looking things. Even though their bark was a strange sound and used to keep me awake sometimes at night. Talking of noises in the dark, the first time I heard the noise cats made when they were squaring up to each other was horrendous. The sound made me think that someone was being Hurt. I ran into Mum and Dad's room, asking what that was, and my dad started to stir. Mum said it was only cats and would tell me about it in the morning. Now I should go before I wake up my dad. I did, but I could still hear them. Andrew said stop getting out of bed, or I will sleep on the floor it stopped after a while with an almighty screech. In the morning, I got up first as it was still unclear what was happening to the cats. Did someone hurt them? Was the fox after them? Mum said when a cat has another cat in the territory of their space, their garden, they make that noise to tell the other to stay away. If one doesn't back down, there is a fight until one cat runs away, normally not the one whose garden it was. That was enough for me; although I did ask if they were still alive, Mum said yes, most times they are, although they might have bits and scratches as fight wounds. That, for some reason, made me smile at war wounds; I thought to show other cats not to mess with me; I wished I were that brave. I once brought a baby hedgehog in when walking back home after being up at my mate Paul's house. The poor little thing was in the gutter at the side of the road, scared it. Nealy got run over by a car as it went past. It went into a ball, so I went to pick it up more out of curiosity than getting it to a safe place at least away from the road, but that is what I would do. It started coming out of its ball and walking into the road again. It felt like I was going to pick it up, and yep, I soon realised that when a Hedgehog is in a ball, the spikes are sharp and very effective at protection. Maybe from my hand, not a car tire, but from my young and stupid hands. I went to grab the little thing; it was only a bit bigger than a tennis ball. bless. I thought it, I'll give it blessed; it was like picking up a load of needles, so as soon as my hand went around it to pick it up, I soon let go. Pinpricks loads of them; I then took my jacket off, as it was cold and frosty that night, and picked it up with that. I still feel the spikes. But instead of putting it under the hedge, I took it home. It was not the smartest idea. As I entered the house, I heard Mum and Dad's door close, the one without the catch. That's good, I thought so I put the hedgehog down on the bottom of the stairs where, as normal, there were loads of shoes and coats on the floor. It took a while to unravel from its ball, but after it did, it ran under a load of coats; I heard Julie and Andrew arguing, so I left Spike's original name, I know, to it. As I went to the kitchen, Mum was getting ready for bed. I knew because she was pouring Dad's cocoa into his cup. Dam, I thought she should be in bed. As she said goodnight, Julie got up to go to bed. On the other hand, Judy was still sitting there, no goodnight from her cow. Just go to bed, I thought. Mum had started up the stairs as Julie got to the bottom stairs. Mum must have disturbed him as he ran out from under the coats. Julie screamed, and I knew why. Mum turned around; I went running toward the hall. Mum said, "It's okay, looking down at Spikey, it's more scared of you than you are of it, standard saying. normally right, though. It is a good job that we didn't live in Africa; I don't suppose the lions would be more scared of me. Julie at once blamed me. Where did I find this? She said too loud. Dad shouted, "What's up? Mum said it's okay; it's only a hedgehog. Dad said to get the flea-ridden thing out of the house. It carries all sorts of diseases. Mum agreed and asked if I had gotten spiked when picking it up. I said no, I had picked it up in my coat. Mum said pick it up in your coat again and put it outside the back. and put the coat on the wash pile and scrub my hands. She didn't want me to have any more time off school; I did as she asked with a big smile. Julie was also smiling at what Mum said about the days off school.

Chapter 14
Away Days

We didn't go on holidays when I was very young, but I remember going on a day trip to Blackpool on the bus Dad had organised with the guys at work. I wasn't very old, maybe 7 or 8, but I remember getting a bright new shiny 50-pence piece, so it must have been after 1971 when the country went Decimal. So, I was over six years old; that was so much money for a young boy like me and was burning a hole in my pocket, as the saying goes. I could not wait to get there. I brought a stick of aniseed rock first, and then Andrew and Julie went into an arcade and played on the machines. Andrew won another few coins, and I thought it was great, so I went to the machine next to him, and before I knew it, all my money was gone. I got upset, and Mum brought me a massive, sweet dummy that I could barely hold in my hands, let alone get it all in my mouth, so I spent most of the next couple of hours watching what the others were doing in the arcade. Then we went down to the beach. We had a ball and some buckets and spades, so we dug a hole to put me in. It seemed fun but took a nasty turn, as it often did. I laid down in the hole with my feet sticking out one end and my head sticking out of the other. Then they started putting sand on top of me. They put more and more sand on me. I started to feel the weight of the sand and started to get a little bit scared. They kept pushing me down. Soon, the sand was too heavy for me to move. The sand on me looked like someone with a huge belly lying on the sand, a beach wale. I thought this made me forget how scared I was for a second or two. but then loads of sand went up my nose and in my mouth. It made me cry. It didn't help that Andrew said we will leave you here, and if the crabs don't get you, the water would, and I would drown. I started to scream. I thought I wasn't going to get out. I thrashed my legs about. Dad looked over from the bar he was at with a couple of his workmates. He said something, but I couldn't hear, because of my screaming, it wasn't Mum that saved me, but a lovely woman that lived in the village and came along with her two young boys around five years old, I think. I would later play with her lads for a while anyway until they moved away. Mum said I'm not getting on the bus like that and took me to the sea to wash me down. Great, I thought as I had a mouth full of salty seawater. I don't know what is worse, the sand or the salty water. Then Mum went back to the arcade to have another go at prize bingo. We all sat in a line and pretended to play. Mum won a few times and got some weird stuff from behind a glass cabinet like it was the crown jewels. We also went in a caravan several times when I was about 13. I remember the site's name: TAGGS Caravan and Camping Site. I would return here later with my girlfriends. These were such special times. one time, my eldest sister, Mary, came, and my youngest sister, Julie, brought my cousin Kate. Now, Kate didn't get out much. She never went anywhere except with her Mum. Until now, she was maybe two years older than Julie, so around 19 years old. Julie and Kate went out as Mary had said, "on the pull," but when they returned, Kate was distraught. She was timid and wouldn't talk to anyone. they were in a bar, and a couple of lads came up to them and started chatting, but one of the guys pointed at Kate and said, "Is she dead?" because she was so scared and shy, she hadn't said a word, Men can be cruel, funny though. This holiday was when I saw one of the most amazing things I have ever seen and one of the most horrific things I've ever seen. I was walking back from the town's seafront with Mary's new man. He was a laugh, but he gambled on the horses, so he didn't last long with Mary. This one day, we stopped to get chips about halfway back to the caravan, as we mostly did. He must have had a win as he brought us all some. Then, in front of me, maybe 50 yards away, it was raining where I stood. It was dry and still bright, but just in front was a wall of water; it was raining so hard you could only see the cars coming through it with their window wipers screeching as they passed as it was dry out of the water wall. Then everyone started running as the rain started moving towards us. Before you knew it, we were soaked and running for dear life to the sanctuary of the caravan. The chips were soggy but got warmed up in the caravan's cooker. I remember how heavy the rain hitting the roof was. We had to shout to hear each other. That wasn't the only rainfall of that holiday; we were all playing on the beach, and I often went to the sea alone. I was safe enough, but what I did love to do was go into the rock pools and find the starfish. I was amazed by them. afternoon, I was in a large rock pool near an old buoy; a few young people were playing there as it was warm, and the water was up to your knees. I left and went back towards the sea when the heavens opened and rained hard. Out of nowhere, there was a lightning strike, and the thunder was deafening. Then, with more lighting strikes, you could hear people shouting and screaming to get out of the water, and off the beach, I saw Mum waving like mad for me to get out of the water. I was running past the buoy when I heard a crack and a scream I had never heard before. It was much louder than the other people shouting; I saw a young girl in the rock pool with me moments earlier, face down with steam coming off her. I didn't know it then, but the lightning struck some breakwater, and the young girl died. Mum told me it could have been you after reading it in the papers the day after, and we went home that day, so we never heard more apart from a small piece on our local news. It was a big thing; there was an inquest, and they shut the beach. I tell myself it all seems like a dream, and maybe it didn't happen.

Chapter 15
Sisters

Many mornings before Joan went to work, when it was so cold, most of us were still at school. You did not want to get out of bed, but one by one, they did. I also had to get up for the tea and toast, then mostly went back to bed when they had all left the house. I think Mary, the eldest, had left by then. We would all try to get in front of the fire to grab what warmth we could, but when Mum shouted Joan, that was pretty much game over. Joan was in her last year of school and did not want to go; what was the point? She was like most of us; we would all fail school exams. she would come down after a while cursing. After calling my Mum all the names under the sun bitch, cow, slag, and lots of others I do not know how to spell, let alone want to repeat, she would push all of us out of the way with a torrent of abuse woe betide anyone that tried to stand their ground, yes I had a go for about 20 seconds. Still, I was so small, and light was pushed out of the way by her. so, after a couple of times, I gave up, but that would wind her up, so that was good; she was so horrible to Mum that she sometimes made her cry. I would try and stick up for Mum, saying stuff like it's not her fault you're a Mardi selfish cow and cannot get out of bed, and with that, mostly would get verbal abuse back, sometimes a slap, then breakfast wait I don't remember much breakfast well-eating breakfast, I remember dad having a fry-up at the weekend Saturday mornings dad didn't like the Ryne of the bacon it was so nice, I didn't always get it dad used to choose the one that could have it sometimes he left a bit of bacon or mushroom bonus I remember whoever got out of bed mum would have a cup of tea and a slice of toast in their hand, it was worth getting out of bed sometimes for even though sometimes the toast was cold, but that was okay it was still strangely nice. every one of us loves tea in the morning, even now. It was probably to get us to sit down and not argue; it didn't work, but she tried. Dad would be able to stop Joan being a bitch, but he never got up before the breakfast mayhem, and they were all starting to get going to school and catch their bus. Mum would go to the local shop and get Dad a "the sun" paper. I liked this as it had page three in it. I think maybe Dad did, too, as when Mum came back, she would shout at him if he weren't down already. He came down and grabbed the paper of whoever was reading it. He hated anyone reading it before him. He would go into the toilet every morning for ages 15 minutes or more. He would then come out, and like there was a special signal or something, the toast appeared for Dad; he got a few rounds, the bread crust, though he wasn't bothered about it. Sometimes, I would get the crust. Oh my blinking gosh, that was so great, and a fresh cup of tea, the day wouldn't get any better than this, but then school. We weren't close as a family and still aren't well. There are different kinds of clicks. Like in a football team, there would be people that stuck together and sat in a group. It was kind of the same for our family. Mary and I always got on, only because when she would come back at weekends to go bingo or visit, I would sometimes get something, sweets mainly. Now, there's a way of getting a little brat off your back. But the biggest ones in those early years were Joan and Dawn. I think because Joan could make Dawn run around and do everything she said, this became stronger throughout their lives, even planning to have children simultaneously or within a few weeks. they had three of them, Joan 3 girls and Dawn 3 boys, which was strange, but all within a few months of each other, so the kids were mostly in the same year at schools. They also went on holiday together, one time even taking me. It was the only time they did, I guess, babysit; I was becoming a more responsible early teenager than not. We all stopped in one caravan or was it two not sure, they only had two each 2 boys and two girls the little ones around 14 moths and the bigger ones around 4 so the last but one day on the holiday Dawn and Joan and their husbands all went out to the cabaret show on the holiday camp but they all went out leaving their youngest two asleep and the middle two just about ready for bed, so we were watching something on the tv just before they went to bed the little ones woke up, and started to cry I was ready for this and began warming there bottles it was going okay until they needed there nappy changing this went okay for the first one but boy the second one was being difficult kept rolling over so I put the first one back into bed she started to cry but I didn't care I still had a change to do the older two came in to see what the noise was, I shut them back into the lounge and proceeded to start the changing I could hear a load of laughter and banging and running around in the other room, you could hear everything in these things only this flimsy sliding door separated us, anyway little Mr. rollie Polli was now changed it was all quite in the other room weird I thought. but put her into bed. They both were exhausted but couldn't sleep, and both made that tired cry; they would never go to sleep because of what I saw when I opened the sliding door. The little darlings had only had the talcum powder out and been chasing each other with it. I couldn't breathe in there, so I shut them into the bit in the middle before the bedrooms, the kitchen area where I changed the little ones. I did my best to sweep the talc with a dustpan and brush, not hover there. Then I heard an almighty noise, thud, slop, bang kind of sound, and went in. The little brats had only tipped over the massive water barrel, which was so big I couldn't carry it when full. Panicking now, I shouted and shoved them into the front room. It was a big mistake; the little ones were crying. The bigger ones were all wet and mixing with what was left of the talc, making a creamy mush all over them and everywhere. About then, my sisters returned and screamed, "What the hell? One went to the little ones, one went to the bigger ones, the three that were left. We had the job of tidying up the mess, which was not easy, and I was not happy wanting to go home, even more than they wanted me to; we only had one more day here, thank God. My eldest sister Mary and her husband haven't been getting on for a while due to his drinking. So, when there was a family wedding, Joan's, I think. The disco and buffet were at the Village Hall, and Mary and her husband stayed at ours. I was on the sofa again, as always if someone stayed over; on the way back to ours, Mary's husband decided to drive the rest of us; it was only A five-minute walk, but he would drive. The problem was he could hardly walk. Mary was screaming at him not to drive. Dad had come out and got home. He turned onto our street and hit a parked car, ripping off the wheel arch and bumper. We got their dad, tried to claim things down, bawled at Mary to get that man in the house, and told us all to go inside. When Dad came back, he had a cut on his head and his arm. where the car owner had picked up the wheel arch and hit Dad with it. That was the last thing that the bloke did. Dad laid him out with one punch, said Andrew, watching from the door. When Dad got home. Mary had put her husband to bed. Good job: they left early the next morning after speaking to Dad. probably to apologise if they had any sense. Not long after that, maybe a year, Mary was alone with her son; he left her, and it was for the best as he was heavy-handed with her. Joan's husband was a bit weird; he thought he knew everything, or so it seemed. I took it all as truth, gullible as they call it. Yes, that's me; once, he said he would give me 50 if he could put a match between my toes and light it. 50p was a lot to me, and I thought about everything I could get. I said without thinking yes, okay, so he put a match in-between my toes, lit a match, and brought it towards the match in my toes. I was panicking inside, and when he lit the match in between my toes, it made me jump, and my foot went up; the match went down; in between, my toes were still alight, and it started to burn. I screamed and started thrashing about. Joan was shouting at him to get it off me at the end. He did, but the match, even though it went out very quickly ma, managed to burn the insides of two of my toes; I was crying. Joan said he was an idiot. He then said I'll give you another 50p if you don't say anything. I took the money and went to bed with a pain in my toes and loads of money in my hand. I did not sleep well for about three days, but spending the money I had earned took me about a week. I earned it the hard way.

Chapter 16
Trouble

Now, this can be a storybook on its own. We would do stuff because we were bored. We didn't do anything major. but There was one time we wanted some food, and the chip shop had loads, so we looked at getting into it. We couldn't get into the front as it was on the main street, and the back door had a solid door on it. But the building was joined to what was a hairdresser; in the back of that was a little room where we went to have our hair cut by a Greek man; every one that went there had pretty much the same haircut. The window to that was open, so in we went. The door to the main hairdresser was easy to force, and we were in; nothing in there apart from a horrible smell. But we did find an attic hatch and climbed up using the chairs, pulling ourselves up. Between the two buildings was a wall with some bricks missing; now we are talking. Paul said, go through there and get some food. So, I climbed halfway through, and I was stuck. very stuck, the remaining bricks were cutting into my sides; if I went back, they cut deeper, and I could feel blood under my shirt. Paul tried to push me, but I couldn't get my hips through. I panicked and swivelled my hips and very badly scratched my sides. My arms were tough, and I couldn't get them back through, so I couldn't go back. I had visions of the next day's paper, the boy caught after getting stuck in the attic. I would never live it down, and I started to cry with panic, screaming at the now-laughing Paul to get me out. As I wriggled, one of the bricks moved; I told him to knock some bricks out so I could get through. He Did. Why the hell didn't we do that first? Anyway, I got through and wouldn't move until he came through. We then found the chip shop's attic hatch hard to open from above; never thought of that, but we did it and dropped down into the chip shop. And there we were, all the frozen pies and all the uncooked chips we could ever want. We tried to warm some up in the microwave. It didn't work well, although we succeeded enough to warm one or two pies to eat. It was still cold in the middle, but we ate them anyway. Then we started throwing a load of chips in a big bucket of water, ready for tomorrow's dinner. We looked at each other rather than at the pies. And the chips on the floor hurt, and people walking by could maybe see us in the back or at least hear us, so we looked at getting back into the attic. We decided we could get out of the back door of the chip shop. from the inside. Another time, we decided to go and get some sweets from the garage. It was a military operation, this one we planned because it had an alarm, or so we thought, and we needed to have our escape route planned out. We couldn't go in the daytime after it had closed; it was on a main road with houses all around, and anyway, they used to leave the light on, so we didn't need torches. We had to keep them down, though. so we planned; we would go around the back and be around there many times after it had closed to look for stuff like an old car tire we could leave in the road or throw in the stream down the road. There were window screens to smash and oil to spill, so we knew what window we would force. We would get some sweets, well, as many as we could in the two bags we brought and go out the same window behind the cars that were for sale, then behind the chippy and hairdressers, cross over towards the place where a lorry and a few buses used to park. Then, behind the cottages through the field that we used to hide from the police in, across a couple of roads, this was the worst bit as we would have to make sure that there wasn't anyone about or walking their dog or any cars coming down the road. Then we would hop over the gate to where the sacred caravan was waiting in the safe place; even if the alarm did go off, we thought we could nail the exit. We got in, and it was surprisingly easy. And the exit was all good, so on our knees, we went into the garage shop. Paul went for the till, but nothing in there. I went the other way to the Cigarette machine and spent all my time ripping the door off; finally, it came off, and there were so many 50 pence pieces as the cigarettes were 50p a pack, so I got a hold of some motorbike gloves that were on sale, a bargain I thought, and with a big smile on my face I put all the 50ps in both gloves I also took a couple of packets of Benson and hedges cigarettes as Mum smoked them, we left the rest all over the floor. Paul, by now, had more sweets and chocolate than he left. time to go, he said; out the window we went, he went first. I passed first the sweets, then the gloves. I had put the cigarettes in the bag with the sweets. As we started our exit route, someone walked by the front of the garage, so we had to hide behind the cars for sale. Everything went fine. We had to wait for two cars on the main road but got to the caravan safely without setting the alarm. That night, we had so many sweets. There was so much chocolate that we couldn't move, so we slept in the caravan anyway. We needed to keep our heads down; we didn't know if they had found out about the garage and what the cops were about. The next morning, we didn't want any of the sweets, definitely no chocolate, so we decided to go into town, maybe stay out and go to a pub, after all, we had quite a bit of money, yeah it was in 50 pence pieces, but it was quite normal to pay with 50p it was enough for most things we would want so Paul went home and got changed, and I would do the same. I waited for him, and we went down to my house. I had all the sweets and chocolates in my pockets he didn't want any more, but I thought I would take a few down to my house as I would get changed. I gave the one glove I was holding to Paul; we had put it in one of the bags with the sweets. We left the rest under every cushion, anywhere we could hide them in a caravan. He was on a peddling bike, if you could call it that. It was the one we used to leave at mine; he would ride it back to his after he went home from mine, or I would ride it to mine after I left his house. Paul rode off down the black pad and saw a police car coming up my street. He kept going and stopping just around the corner to watch the cop car. As I came out of the black pad to the top of my street, the police car, which I didn't know was there, was just about to turn around and stop. Andy left the passenger side and said your Mum had put a missing person out for you; she hasn't seen you for a week (sleeping in the caravan, that's why, I thought). Dam, why now? Why, today, she has never put a missing person out for me ever. But I wasn't going to stand there and call him a liar. Then I said I'm going there now, and he said, we will give you a lift; I panicked. In a tiny and scared voice, I said the house was just there and pointed. I can see my house. I said, and he said, "I know where you live." I will drop you down and have a word with your Mum. And with that, he opened the rear of the cop car. I looked over to where Paul was; the sheer look of panic in his eyes was striking. I saw him fly down the street, throwing the bag over someone's hedge; while I was getting into the back seat, luckily, Andy didn't see him. He went down to the bottom of the road and waited to see what would happen.

We didn't move in the cop car for ages as Andy asked Questions like, "Where were you last night? "Down the park", I said all night "Yes", "then slept around my mate's house." "Paul," said Andy. "Maybe", I said, shuffling nervously. As I did, a few packets of sweets fell out of my pocket; Shit had Andy seen them, I thought. Yep, "and where did they come from? "Andy" said. I have just brought them; I said, "Empty your pockets. "Andy said, the game was up. I had to show him everything and got arrested. Paul got arrested. Even the kid who found a glove full of money in his front garden was questioned for hours to ensure he had nothing to do with it. (He told us later that his dad had taken some of the money before telling the police that his son had found it on the lawn.) I had to tell them about the caravan; that was the worst part. Paul and I had to go to Court and got 120 hours of Community service each. Still, we couldn't do it simultaneously, so he had to do it on some Saturdays. I had to do mine on a Sunday, but we still hung about together to get into more trouble. The thing with doing community service was you could do anything. Paul had to paint mostly, and I did some painting. Still, there was one time I had to go to a correction school because I missed the pick-up to do the painting, gardening, or whatever they had us do. The correction school is where you have training like the Army; it was horrendous. It is an ancient building with four floors; I am sure you wouldn't get away with it now, but the guy in charge was an ex-marine and a bit strange. He wore very tight shorts and liked to keep us just in our trousers, no socks and shoes, and no tops allowed for the first 20 minutes. So that he could look at your toe and fingernails, he would put his fingers in between your toes, spread them apart, and see if there was any dirt or fluff between them. If any of us had dirty fingers or toenails, he would make us do twenty push-ups, and if you couldn't do them, everyone had to do twenty. You were standing there with hardly anything on in the middle of winter in a big hall freezing. But you couldn't move until he told you to go ahead; you could not scratch your nose; if you did, he would make you do twenty press-ups; every week, someone would get picked on until he couldn't do any more push-ups. Then we all had to do them. Sometimes, he would let us put our clothes on. Occasionally, we had to pick them up and run to the changing room, where he would watch us all get changed. The last one changed into shorts, and a t-shirt you brought would get twenty push-ups. I discovered you couldn't have them on under your trousers. If you did, you would get twenty push-ups. If you were last out into the courtyard down three flights of stairs, with Sergeant Major or whatever he thought he was, screaming behind you, move it. Faster. Trying not to fall on the stone staircase or get pushed, lots of cuts going down those stairs; one lad had to go with one of the police officers; yeah, they were around, too. He never came back. They said he broke his arm. When you got outside, you had to stand to attention just like in the Army, so if you were last at playing soldier, you had to drop and give him twenty press-ups, whatever the weather. We would march around the yard, turn right, stamp our feet, turn left quickly, march, stand at ease, then pay attention, slamming our feet down; the last one had to, yes, do twenty press-ups. That guy couldn't do it by now, so we all had to do some most weeks. Then we went into the gym on the third floor and had to do fitness training. There were ropes to climb benches to walk along without falling off, running races, sit, star jumps, and push-ups like we didn't know how to do them. There was a ball tig where you had to throw a ball, and if it hit you, you had to grab a ball and hit someone else. The worst part was the wrestling; it was okay the first five times I went as I was in the same age group under 18s, but because there wasn't a bus from my village early enough. To get me into the school, and I was always late. They made me go into the under-20s now. Some big lads were in this group, so everything was much more challenging—especially the wrestling. I got hurt a few times as I wasn't the biggest of the boys. I wasn't the biggest in the under-18s. But at least he knew I tried and left me alone mostly. He had his favourites. But he only made the younger lads go into the yard with their pants if they forgot their shorts, never the older ones. I got through it in the end.

Chapter 17
Driving

Paul and I used to do lots of things together, even stealing the odd car for a joyride. Once, we had a little drive in a Ford or something or other, and Paul was quite a good driver. We went driving for around half an hour. Because there was not much fuel in it, we went back to our village, so we did not have to walk home; we found close to two pounds worth of change in the car and wanted to get back before the shop shut, Paul said we could make it back at the traffic lights corner of the village we ran out of petrol luckily managed to pull it onto a curb and as we went up the Curb it caused the car to get stuck on the bollard or something there was a very bad scraping then crunch sound as the car stopped. We ran, but we hid from every vehicle we saw coming as we couldn't tell if it was the police. As it was dark, all we could see were headlights on that dark stretch of road. We got to the shop and celebrated with about one pound of sweets each. I said in the shop Happy birthday, so if the shopkeeper was wondering where we got the money, it seemed clever. It wasn't just Paul and cars. I got confident in the driving lessons around a massive car park; Andrew used to take me and let me drive his car. I was getting good, or so I thought. Sometimes, he let me drive Dad's van, not when he was with us. Once, I went around a corner too wide on a country lane, and the car coming the other way made me panic. I steered to the left too much and ended up with two wheels on the grass verge, bouncing up and down like a spring that has forgotten how to stop. Andrew told me to stop, and we switched over; he drove but did say I Did okay but needed to keep an eye on where I was on the road all the time. I moved more and more and had a few lessons. Dad even let me drive with him to the builder's merchant and once on my own to take a load of earth to Andrews's flat at the top of the road. We got it when digging out on a slabbing job that day. It was going fine, but it was never going to end well. It never seemed to end well around that time; I had to turn in the road and then reverse to his fence, so I started reversing up to Andrews Garden fence so we could unload out the back of the van. It was going well.

Andrew was waving to me to keep coming back. I could see him in my mirrors. Until I could not see him anymore, I kept going backwards; Andrew, though, had seen his new Girlfriend coming down the black pad they cut through at the top of our road. So, I kept coming and coming, not knowing that I had hit a car and started pushing it down the road towards Andrew's flat. The owner came running out and started banging on the van. By this time, Andrew had also returned, opened the door, and screamed, "Stop, you have hit a car. My car said the man. Andrew then said we would sort it out. Don't worry; I'll give you all the details; then he said he knew who we were and knew that I hadn't gotten a license, let alone insurance, but I told Andrew you weren't driving, I'd get dad. He said yeah, you best do, Dad went up and sorted it out, but the cops came around even though Dad gave him money to pay for it. Dad had words later. With the car owner, this time, I don't think Dad was so accommodating. I went to Court and had to pay damages to his car even though Dad had given him money; I now know Dad's word was to give me back the money I gave you because he said he called the cops a fine for no insurance. And points on my license even before I had one; the judge said if I ever drove without being fully legal and having a full driving license, I would go to prison. Dad never let me drive his van again. After his car, I was surprised he let me drive anything of his ever.

Chapter 18
Graveyard Tig

There are some strange games kids used to play. One of our favourite pastimes was playing night-time tig in the graveyard. It was perfect; it had a gate on one side of the church and a gate at the other with gravestones all around it. It was so dark there, and we used to play it with the older kids. Andrew was playing it once, and that's how we would join. but there were some rules. One was it wouldn't start until midnight, and the last one through the gate at 1 minute passed would be the chaser. Or one would be chosen from the last through; it was me once, and it was horrible that things were making noises and moving in the corner of your eye. shadows everywhere; one time, there was a cat, or it may have been a rat, but either way, it scared me, and I ran to one of the gates. Luckily, I caught one of the guys, so it stopped me from running home. I did catch six of them. There was the one still to catch, they said was the best. he was good; I never caught him, and few did. He shouted at me from the other side of the gate. yeah, yeah, okay, you did it again one of the older boys shouted. We never really had time for more than one game as three houses around the churchyard would call the police, mostly because someone set their light sensor off or the old gits would wait to see if we were there. Still, mostly, the cops came around looking anyway. Every time the cops caught up with us on something, they would warn us to stop doing it, as anyone caught there after midnight would spend the night in jail. Though it never happened,' it came close. They appeared at the bridge side of the church, and yes, we all ran through the other gate. never caught any of us, not in the church anyway. Oh, there are lots of memories of the older kids. What they sometimes did was unbelievable; they used to block the crossroads and get one of our younger ones to call the police from the phone box. I did it once, and you had to ring 999 and did not need any ten pence for that. and in a panicky voice, said there were loads of teenagers in the middle of the crossroads, completely blocking all the traffic coming in all directions. My dad told me to run down the phone box and call the police; after they asked me where and how many, I would put the phone down as the next question would be what's your name. yeah, okay, I will give them that, not! The people in the cars wouldn't do anything as there were loads of kids; if any did try and say something, they would get loads of abuse and things thrown at them and their cars; most would drive by sounding their horn, we all loved that and cheered when it happened. The cops always came. Andy was always with them. The other police officer would come. We were all ready for them and would always disperse in various directions. Sometimes, they would chase some on the mopeds, or sometimes, they would chase the ones running down the main street. Or up station road. This one time, there were three cop cars. They came from everywhere. Two chased the mopeds, and we saw one guy fall his bike off as he went up a curb that Copper had got his man. One of the cars chased us down the main street; there were about six of us, and we all knew where we were heading for the field just after the cottages and before the parade of shops on the other side of the field where a new building site was. In this field was long, dense grass at least a meter tall. And we would all hide in it. The cop car had a kind of searchlight on the top of it, I suppose, a car that went to accidents and could light up the scene. Wow, that thing was bright. It went from left to right across the field. and sometimes, one of us would run from where they were and dive into the grass. When the light came towards him, there were two ways out of the field. a high fence towards the building site and one where the cops were. Three left the field at the building site with the high fence. with the searchlight just too late to see them. The other one was where the cop cars were on the main street. Some tried to make a run for it, three got caught, and one got away, but that meant the car on the main street went after him. We stayed hidden for a few minutes when the coast was clear. It was the best fun we had in ages. That was a bit scary, and we both thought Andy would catch up with us for it, but he didn't; I suppose he was just happy getting the three or maybe four if he got the one running. The other police car was still on the lookout for the mopeds. We saw one chasing one going past the bottom of my street. The moped we knew would turn up a small road just after my street. The police car with the blues and two's blaring followed him as we ran up to the top of our road to where that road joined mine. The council had put three bollards at the top to stop people from using it as a cut-through. this police officer did not know, and away the moped went beeping his horn. Paul and I were cheering and putting up the V sign to the coppers in the car. It was not Andy; he would not have gone up there as he was local. good times. It was always fun to hear that people had got one over on the police.

Chapter 19
Love

Love comes in many different forms; I was never horrible to anyone or anything, but it never got me the girl. If there was a spider in the house, Andrew was scared and would try to squash it; I would never even think about killing it; I would catch it and put it outside: the cats, the dogs, the birds. I would even feed them a few times. I used to go to an after-school class. It was all about bird watching, mainly because one of the best-looking girls in the school smiled at me once, so I went, but I soon realised that she loved birds more than me, well, anything more than me. So that after-school activity soon stopped, but it never stopped me dreaming about her for months, mainly about the teacher talking and talking, and we would slip into the bushes and start kissing. Then, I would generally wake up, never knowing how that dream ended. Apart from fancying many girls, I never had the confidence to talk to them, probably because of all the name-calling about my big ears and the fact that I was a coward and weak. My first kind of love was at one of my sister's birthday parties. This girl called Lorraine was so pretty that I could not take my eyes off her. She knew I was staring and looking away whenever she looked at me. I found out, kept smiling at me. Mary told me her name and that she was her babysitter. I was into her big time; I fell into her eyes; she was so pretty. With my teenage hormones all over the place, I didn't know what to say; I wanted to talk to her so badly. Mary knew this, and so did Larraine, it Turned out. She came over to me after Mary had said something to her. Amazingly, I started to speak to her and asked her if my nephew was as much of a pain for her as he was for me when I looked after him. even though I never looked after him. She said no, always fine for me, she said and smiled. Mary heard and said he fancies you, that's why. I said I could see why, got embarrassed, and went to the bar. I turned around and noticed her smiling, not just smiling. She was smiling at me. And with a bit of colour in her cheeks as well. But that made her look even more lovely, I thought. I shouldn't drink any more, but I got two lagers, one for me and one for Lorraine. I started to drink it relatively quickly because I was nervous and was running out of things to say. She didn't want her drink, so I had that as well. But as soon as I had finished it, I felt so ill. I shouldn't mix drinks, I found out that night. Beer with Gin and tonic don't mix (not with me anyway), my stomach churning, dizziness, and blurred vision. I had to get outside, needed air, and had to leave there so Lorraine wouldn't see; I went out, sat on some stairs and was violently sick everywhere. I didn't know it initially, only after I had stopped being sick. Lorraine was there with me. She was moving my hair from my face and stroking my back, and with the sweatiest, most caring-sounding voice I had ever heard, she said you would be okay, you know, don't worry. It happens to the best of us. I wanted to stay and kiss her for a moment, but how could I? There were still some pieces of sick in my mouth. I was still very embarrassed and got up to walk home; she said are you okay I said yes, I think so. I can help if you like. I heard my stupid mouth say no, you're alright. Go back in and enjoy yourself. I was okay and walked away, feeling the most embarrassed I had ever felt; I never saw Lorraine again.

I tried. I just wanted to say I wish I had stayed that night and held you in my arms like you did me, looking into the diamonds that were your eyes, kissed you, and thanked you for being there when I needed someone to care for me. Mary never had a phone, so I couldn't contact her to tell Lorraine; I never stopped thinking about her. It must have been a month later when Mary came over the next time. I asked her where she lived, and Mary told me she had moved; she said she had lost contact with her. I said you must be able to talk to her Mum and dad; how did you find her to ask her to babysit? She said it was a couple at the pub where she used to work; it was their daughter. Mary said it was a shame because she was the best babysitter she had ever had. Soon, Mary would also move, so there was no chance of finding her. Mary got a new babysitter. So, I never tracked her down. I am so stupid, and I regret it to this day. It wasn't long before I found the love of my life, but I had to get through school first.

These are my memories as I remember them.

And may not be the exact way it happened.

More expected from this author

Should I have Turned Right

My life in a letter volume 2

My life in a letter volume 3

Love, life, live, die.

Printed in the United States
by Baker & Taylor Publisher Services